Greek Mythology: Kingdom of Hades

GREEK MYTHOLOGY SERIES
BY MICHAEL J DEFOSSE

Greek Mythology: Gods of Mount Olympus
Myths, Powers, and Legends That Shaped Ancient Greece

Greek Mythology: Kingdom of Hades
Underworld Myths, Chthonic Gods, and the Secrets of the Dead

COMING SOON

Greek Mythology: Dominion of Poseidon
Myths of Sea Gods, Ocean Monsters, and Ancient Legends of the Deep

Greek Mythology: Rise and Fall of the Titans
Primordial Gods, Titan Myths, and the Battle for the Cosmos

Greek Mythology: Illustrated Companion Guide
Gods, Heroes, Symbols, and Creatures of Ancient Greece

STEP INTO THE REALM OF GODS,
BEASTS, AND LEGENDS —
WHERE MYTH BREATHES ETERNAL

Receive future book updates and news:
info@mythologypublishing.com

GREEK MYTHOLOGY: KINGDOM OF HADES

UNDERWORLD MYTHS, CHTHONIC GODS, AND THE SECRETS OF THE DEAD

BY MICHAEL J DEFOSSE

Mythology Publishing

GREEK MYTHOLOGY: KINGDOM OF HADES

For inquiries, contact Mythology Publishing at:
info@mythologypublishing.com

ISBN: 979-8-9997003-3-9 (Paperback)
ISBN: 979-8-9997003-5-3 (Hardcover)

Library of Congress Control Number: Pending
First Edition
10 9 8 7 6 5 4 3 2 1

Printed in the United States of America
Published in New York, NY

DEDICATION

To the curious explorers of ancient myths and timeless
legends—

To those who find wonder in hidden realms and fascination
in the stories of the afterlife—

To every reader who has ever imagined the winding paths
of the Underworld and the mysteries of Hades' domain—

This book is dedicated to you.

May these tales illuminate the rich tapestry of Greek
mythology, offering a glimpse into a world where shadows
and light intertwine, and legends come to life.

Thank you for joining me on this journey through the
stories of the Underworld and beyond.

SCROLLS OF OLYMPUS

PREFACE

To the ancient Greeks, death was not an end but a passage. Beneath the surface of the earth stretched a twilight dominion. Solemn, silent, and unyielding. This was the Underworld—a realm not of chaos or fire, but of consequence, where every soul was bound to a law, older than Olympus itself.

Every culture has wondered what becomes of love when the body fails—the Greeks answered with a kingdom built of memory.

Here ruled Hades, the unseen sovereign, austere yet just. He was no monster, but a guardian of order, ensuring each spirit found its destined place. At his side stood Persephone, Queen of Shadows and of Spring, whose descent and return wove the eternal rhythm of death and renewal, sorrow and bloom.

Greek Mythology: Kingdom of Hades is more than a descent into myth—it is a guided journey into the hallowed architecture of the afterlife, mapped by rivers of memory, guarded by spectral powers, and shaped by oaths no god could break.

The gates now stand open—beyond the unseen threshold lies the kingdom of silence and veil.

Step forward…the journey has begun.

INTRODUCTION

Passage to the Underworld

For as long as mortals have gazed into the night sky and questioned the meaning of their breath, they have also pondered what lies beyond the final exhale. To the ancient Greeks, death did not bring oblivion, but passage—a descent into a cloaked dusk beneath the surface of the earth. This was the Underworld, a shadowed kingdom of gloaming and silence, where the souls of the departed began their eternal voyage. It was not a pit of torment, but a domain of order and solemn justice, governed by Hades with unwavering solemnity.

> "Do not seek to know what fate the gods have given;
> be wise, strain the wine, for life is brief.
> While we speak, envious time has fled: seize the day,
> trusting as little as possible in the future."
> — Horace, *Odes*

Unlike the disordered imaginings of other afterlife traditions, where reward and ruin blur without rule, the Greek vision of the afterlife was one of sacred architecture. It was a place of consequence, shaped by celestial justice and the moral weight of a soul's deeds. Here, destiny unfolded not by whim, but by the measured hands of the Fates, judges, and guardians of the twilight realm.

Within these pages, we descend together into the mythic depths of the Greek Underworld. We will uncover its sovereign gods and spectral guardians, traverse its mystical rivers and murky groves, and recount the legends of heroes and mortals who dared to defy the boundary between the living and the dead.

TWILIGHT KINGDOM

To the ancient Greeks, death did not mark an end, but a passage—an inevitable crossing from the reach of sunlight into the hidden domain of veil. The Underworld stood not in opposition to life, but as its silent counterpart, a hallowed continuation where the mortal thread was weighed and woven anew. Unlike later visions that splinter the afterlife into paradise and perdition, the ancient Greek version was a single, unified kingdom, vast and layered, its regions shaped not by divine whim, but by the soul's own deeds and destiny.

This chthonic domain mirrored the complexities of mortal existence. It was neither wholly dark nor wholly just and it offered no simplistic binaries of reward or damnation. Some souls found rest in the Elysian Fields, touched by golden light and eternal harmony. Others were cast into the pale shade, their grief echoing through the desolate plains of Asphodel. And many, neither cursed nor exalted, drifted in the gray hush of unremarkable eternity.

To die was not a tragedy. It was truth. The Greeks embraced this with reverent ritual, binding death to honor and order. Funeral rites were sacred obligations, for an unburied soul was believed to wander, lost and voiceless, denied passage to the afterlife. A coin placed beneath the tongue served as payment to Charon, the solemn ferryman who rowed the dead across the black waters of the River Styx. Without it, a spirit lingered in limbo, caught forever between worlds—unmourned, unrested, and unseen.

FATE AND SHADOW

Far more than a resting place for the dead, the Underworld stood as a living pillar in the architecture of Greek myth, a land

4

where fate converged, truth was unveiled, and the immortal and mortal alike were tested. It was a place of reckoning and revelation, a sacred crucible where heroes journeyed not merely to confront death, but to seek wisdom, redemption, or the impossible return of a lost soul.

Within its darkened passageways, Orpheus played his lyre to summon love from beyond the mist. Heracles wrestled the hound of Hades in pursuit of immortality. Odysseus stood among the shades, gleaning prophecy from the lips of the dead. Each fall into darkness was more than a trial—it was a confrontation with destiny itself.

Here too reigned Persephone, Queen of the Dead, her presence a living paradox. A daughter of spring, sovereign of shadow. Her myth wove together the rhythms of harvest and decay, illuminating the eternal transformation between light and darkness, birth and burial.

Justice, not chaos, governed this chthonic realm. Souls faced the echo of their deeds, judged and assigned to their proper place—rewarded, punished, or simply remembered. Even the gods bowed to its power, for any oath sworn upon the River Styx was sacred and binding, sealed in waters no deity dared betray.

WHISPERS BEYOND THE DIVIDE

This book offers an odyssey, not into darkness alone, but into wonder. It is a guided journey through one of the most mysterious and evocative areas in all Greek mythology, the Kingdom of Hades. Within these pages, readers will uncover the ancient myths and hallowed legends that shaped how the Greeks understood death—

not as an end, but as a transformation shaped by godlike law and cosmic design.

They will encounter the chthonic gods who ruled the depths, the spirits who wandered between silence and darkness, and the monstrous guardians who stood sentinel at the edges of oblivion. They will explore how these figures were not merely tales, but reflections of belief, fear, and reverence—woven into rituals, oaths, and the moral structure of Greek society.

By journey's end, readers will hold a deeper understanding of how the ancient Greeks perceived the soul's fate, the balance of justice after death, and the unseen threads that bound the mortal world to the gods. Through immersive storytelling and mythic insight, this book seeks not only to inform, but to awaken awe, ignite curiosity, and honor the enduring mystery of the world beyond.

Through the Underworld

This book unfolds as a guided descent, each chapter a torchbearer illuminating a different facet of the shrouded depths. Like the steps of an ancient ritual, each section leads deeper into the mysteries of the Greek Underworld, revealing its gods, its geography, its myths, and its lasting grip upon the soul of human imagination.

We begin at the throne of Hades, the silent king of the dead. His origins, powers, and solemn dominion are uncovered in full, revealing a god not of cruelty, but of order, balance, and inescapable fate. From there, we turn to Persephone, the radiant Queen, whose abduction and evolution gave birth to the cycle of death and renewal, echoing in every season.

The journey continues into the very terrain of the Underworld. We trace the dark rivers that carve its borders, passing through gates that sever the living from the dead, and walk the paths where souls are judged and divided—toward blissful rest, eternal wandering, or unending torment. Along the way, we meet the divine arbiters who weigh a soul's worth and oversee its destiny.

Legends of mortals who dared to breach the depths also take their place. Heroes like Orpheus, Heracles, and Odysseus all walk these pages, their quests through the Underworld revealing truths about courage, loss, and the human yearning for second chances.

In the final chapters, we step beyond myth to witness the enduring legacy. We explore how these ancient beliefs shaped ritual, inspired generations of poets and painters, and continue to cast long shadows over modern tales of death and the afterlife.

By journey's end, you will possess a deep and vivid understanding of the Greek Underworld, its divine rulers, spectral landscapes, and the stories that still stir the hearts of those who dare to look beyond the mortal curtain.

ECHOES BEYOND THE VEIL

The vision of the Underworld did not fade with the fall of Greece. From the marble tombs of Athens to the catacombs of Rome, its shadow endured—reborn in verse, art, and the quiet philosophies that questioned what follows the final breath. The poets of antiquity carried its echoes across centuries; Homer's spirits in the halls of Hades, Virgil's descent through the gates of Dis, Dante's vast inferno built upon their foundations. Each age reimagined the kingdom below, shaping it to reflect its own fears and hopes.

To the Romans, it became a mirror of empire—ruled not by chaos, but by order. To the early philosophers, it was an allegory of the soul's journey toward understanding. Even as faiths shifted and new heavens rose, the Greeks' shadowed realm of consequence remained. It whispered through monastic visions, medieval carvings, and Renaissance canvases where angels and shades traded places across the boundary of salvation and memory.

Though the centuries turned and reason replaced reverence, the image of Hades' realm refused to die. It persisted not because men feared darkness, but because they recognized themselves within it. The Underworld endures because it names what cannot be erased. Remembrance, judgment, and love's last echo. It is not a fantasy of punishment, but an architecture of meaning—a reflection of how deeply the living long to understand their own impermanence.

What would you see, if you stood before those gates?

Perhaps you would find that the vision endures not in ancient shrines, but within the private myth each mortal carries—the instinct to measure a life, to weigh what was given and what was kept. Even now, the gates stand open in thought and art, in every elegy whispered to the dead, in every hope that the soul might outlast the dust.

For myth, like memory, cannot die. It waits beyond time's horizon, where the voices of the old world still call through the veil—reminding us that death was never the enemy, only the mirror. And beyond that mirror, unseen yet eternal, the throne of silence remains.

CHAPTER 1

HADES

King of the Dead

Hades' story is etched in destiny, shaped by fate, and forged in the cosmic upheaval that gave rise to the Olympian order. Though he would come to rule the dead with solemn authority, the path began in chaos, born to a world teetering on the edge of ruin. He was imprisoned in darkness by a father gripped by fear, yet from that confinement, Hades emerged as a force of spiritual purpose. The dark monarch played a pivotal role in the war that shattered the age of Titans and helped carve the world into three sacred domains. His was the kingdom beneath all others—the Underworld, a land of silence, judgment, and eternal passage. To grasp the nature of this chthonic sovereign, one must first trace the forces that forged him.

> *"There is a land called Hades' House,*
> *A realm of mist and gloom,*
> *No sun ever shines upon its mournful shore,*
> *But it stretches in eternal shadow."*
> — Homer, *Odyssey*

Born of Darkness

Long before he claimed his throne in the mystical depths, Hades was born into a world on the brink of collapse, a child of the Titans, Cronus and Rhea, fated to rise from darkness. Like his siblings—Hestia, Demeter, Hera, and Poseidon—the arrival of the future king of the dead was met not with celebration, but with apprehension. Gripped by fear of a prophecy foretelling his fall, Cronus devoured each child at birth, sealing them in the silent prison of his own body. Thus, Hades' earliest existence unfolded in absolute darkness, a prophecy in embryo of the realm he would one day command.

The will of fate, though delayed, cannot be denied. With the secret birth of Zeus, hidden away by Rhea in defiance of Cronus' fear, the tide began to turn. Zeus grew to strength in obscurity, and when the time came, he rose in open rebellion. The future king of Olympus forced his father to disgorge the swallowed gods, and from this act of deliverance, the great war was born. The Titanomachy raged for ten years, shaking the heavens and scorching the earth with the fury of the gods.

In the chaos of this war, Hades proved himself not by thunder or tempest, but by stealth and strategy. Armed with the Helm of Darkness, a gift from the Cyclopes, the silent one moved unseen across the battlefield, a deathly force in the struggle for cosmic order. With each unseen strike, he helped turn the tide against the Titans. When the final blow was struck and the old gods cast into Tartarus, Hades stood alongside his brothers, poised to divide the cosmos. From that moment, the world would be ruled by three thrones; one in the sky, one as part of the sea, and one in the darkness below.

Dividing the Cosmos

With the Titans imprisoned in the abyss, the three Olympian brothers—Zeus, Poseidon, and Hades—stood at the dawn of a new order, faced with the celestial task of dividing the cosmos among themselves. The sons of Cronus drew lots beneath the gaze of fate itself, each accepting what destiny decreed.

The sky was to be ruled by Zeus, whose thunder would command the heavens while the seas surged under the trident of

Poseidon. And to Hades came the unseen kingdom below, the vast reaches of the Underworld, where mortal souls journeyed after death. Though some have mistaken this as a grim or lesser fate, the myths speak of no bitterness in Hades' acceptance. It was a role not of punishment, but of solemn necessity.

Unlike his brethren, whose presence stirred the storms and kindled the drama of Olympus, Hades did not seek ambition beyond the depths beneath the earth. The king of the dead did not thunder across the skies or rise in wrath from the ocean's tides. Instead, he governed the Underworld with quiet power—unshaken, just, and absolute. While Zeus ruled over celestial law and Poseidon shaped the seas with fury and force, Hades upheld the rhythm of life, death, and what lay beyond. His was a throne carved not of ambition, but of destiny—an inheritance written in shadow.

Often mistaken for the god of death itself, Hades held a role far more sacred. That mantle belonged to Thanatos, the very personification of death's touch. Hades did not steal breath, he received it. He was not a harvester of souls, but their final custodian. As keeper of souls, Hades ensured that all who crossed into his realm were judged, placed, and remembered. His laws were eternal and his rule stern, yet the arbiter of death was never unjust.

Oaths of the Styx

Although the god of the Underworld ruled far from the halls of Mount Olympus and rarely interfered in the squabbles of other gods and mortals, his authority extended beyond the boundaries of death. In the jurisdiction of sacred oaths and supreme contracts, none carried greater weight than Hades himself. Among the immortals, promises were not mere words but cosmic bindings, and none were more solemn than those sworn upon the River Styx.

The Styx, one of the five rivers that veined the Underworld, was more than a pathway to the next world. It was a primordial force, a current of truth itself. To swear upon its waters was to stake one's providence on the unbreakable. Even Zeus, king of the gods, was subject to its power. Should a god or deity violate such an oath, the punishment was severe, and could dictate exile, silence, and heavenly disgrace. The River Styx bound even the highest of gods to the laws that flowed from the Kingdom of Shadows.

Within this framework of eternal law, Hades stood as its unflinching guardian. While Zeus issued celestial commands and Poseidon shook the earth and sea, Hades upheld a deeper justice, one untouched by persuasion or pity. In his kingdom, the rules were not subject to favor. All who entered his world, even the gods, were bound by its laws and where oaths met the threshold of death, Hades ensured they were honored or punished with perfect precision.

One of the most haunting examples of such unbreakable law is found in the myth of Orpheus and Eurydice. When the mortal bard descended into the Hidden Kingdom and moved Hades and Persephone with his grief-laden song, they granted him a rare gift. Eurydice could return, but only if Orpheus walked ahead and never looked back at her until they had left the Underworld. This was no simple condition. It was an unalterable contract, forged in sorrow and sealed by the will of the veiled realm. When Orpheus faltered and turned too soon, the bond was broken. Eurydice vanished, and Hades, though not uncaring, did not intervene. The laws had been broken. The land of the dead had spoken, and it does not echo twice.

Keeper of the Final Truth

Among the Greek gods, none was more misunderstood than Hades. The hidden one stood apart in a silent, watchful, and unwavering existence. He did not meddle in mortal lives for sport, nor did he crave war or expansion of his dominion. Yet, his name was spoken in whispers, his presence feared more than that of any other celestial deity.

This fear did not rise from acts of evil or cruelty, but from the solemn power he embodied. Hades was the keeper of souls—the unreturning, the unseen. In a world where death was both certain and mysterious, the king of the Underworld became the living reminder of that which mortals most dreaded. While other gods ruled over sky and storm, harvest and hearth, Hades reigned over the final truth. The unyielding thread of destiny that awaited all. To speak his name was to confront mortality, and few did so willingly.

Yet fear should not be mistaken for villainy. Neither a tormentor, nor devil of later faiths, Hades was the custodian of order. His divine duty was not to punish, but to preserve and the keeper of souls governed the afterlife with justice and restraint. His sovereignty was an ordered kingdom where the departed found their rightful end and oaths held the weight of eternity.

Even in myths where his presence feels severe, a closer gaze reveals fairness beneath the veil. In the tale of Persephone, where he takes her from the land of the living, Hades is often cast as an abductor. Yet in the Underworld, Persephone does not remain captive, but rises as Queen of the Underworld, a sovereign equal. Hades never betrayed her, nor did he seek another. Unlike Zeus with his endless liaisons or Poseidon with his storms of passion, Hades was loyal, constant in love as in rule.

Few dared to raise temples in his name, yet his presence was never absent. Mortals honored him with distance and reverence, not scorn. For they knew his place in the cosmic order was ordained. He upheld the cycle of life and death, safeguarded the passage of souls, and enforced the laws none dared to break. Hades was a guardian of balance, the still hand at the edge of existence, ensuring that all things, in time, returned to their proper place.

THE UNSEEN POWER

Hades' dominion was elemental, sustaining the balance between life and death. His authority, absolute within the Underworld, extended through divine law, hidden wealth, and the unbreakable power of sacred oaths. With the Helm of Darkness, Hades became a phantom, invisible even to gods, striking unseen and enforcing order without spectacle. The King of the Underworld ruled without spectacle or display. He governed the unseen; buried riches, unspoken truths, and the fate of every soul. Unlike his tempestuous kin, Hades ruled with restraint, embodying cosmic balance over violence. The ruler of the chthonian gods was not thunder nor tide, but simply silence, law, and consequence. In every oath sworn, in every soul judged, the power of Hades moved, unseen but unchallenged.

> *"But upon all men, both good and bad,*
> *comes death alike, and not even the gods*
> *can save a man they love,*
> *when deadly fate lays hold upon him."*
> — Homer, *Iliad*

Master of the Final Gate

To mortals dwelling under the golden sun of Greece, the Underworld was a realm of mystery, a place veiled in silence, unreachable by the living. But to Hades, it was a kingdom, a burden, and a sacred trust —his realm, solemn and inviolate. The sovereign of the unseen presided over the one domain no mortal could escape. His domain did not pulse with storms or song, but with ordained certainty. Death came for all, and Hades received each soul with solemn grace. Though feared, his domain was not chaos—it was ordered, bound by ancient law, and held together by the will of its ruler.

The warden of souls was not the judge of the departed. That duty belonged to the three Judges of the Dead—Minos, Rhadamanthus, and Aeacus—who measured the worth of each life. Yet it was Hades who ensured those judgments endured. The domain of the dead, vast and layered, held firm boundaries; the gray Asphodel Meadows, the blissful Elysian Fields, and the abyss of Tartarus. Each soul was assigned its due, and none left without reason. His law was not vengeance, but permanence.

Even the gods hesitated to breach his gates and few mortals ever dared the path back to life. Among the few was Orpheus, whose song moved even the heart of Hades. Moved by his music, the god granted a fragile mercy where Eurydice might return, but only if Orpheus led without turning. When he faltered, the law held firm. There were no second chances in the realm of the dead. Not even love could rewrite its decree.

Despite the gloom cast by his name, Hades was a force of cosmic balance. He ensured that the living did not hoard the dead and that the dead did not roam among the living. His authority upheld the boundary between worlds—absolute, unyielding, and sacred. In a universe ruled by chaos and change, Hades alone preserved what could not be undone. Yet even before his rule of souls began, the symbol of his dominion had been forged in fire and silence.

Lord of Hidden Wealth

Though mortals feared Hades as lord of the dead, they also knew a deeper truth buried beneath that fear. Gold veins, silver seams, and jewels forged in the dark were his treasures by right. To the Greeks, he was not only Hades but Plouton (Wealthy One), a name that echoed through time and later became Pluto, his Roman incarnation.

Unlike the fortunes of sky or sea, Hades' wealth was silent, immutable, and eternal. It did not crash like waves or vanish like clouds, but remained buried, locked in stone, untouched by time. Just as souls entered his realm and never returned, so too did the riches of the earth remain sealed within his domain. Miners, blacksmiths, and those who sought fortune from the depths often invoked his name, not in fear, but in solemn hope that the god of the chthonic domain might grant them favor.

Yet the riches of the earth, like death itself, were never to be seized lightly. Myths tell of mortals who dug too deep or defied the gods in pursuit of the earth's hidden bounty, only to be cursed or struck down. The message was clear. Prosperity could be a blessing, but when pursued with greed or irreverence, it became a path into ruin. The treasures of Hades were hallowed, and to claim them unjustly was to invite doom.

And yet Hades himself was untouched by avarice. Unlike other gods who meddled in mortal ambition, he remained distant, unmoved by power or pleasure. His wealth was not a trophy, but a truth—quiet, enduring, and absolute. The master of the final gate did not crave more, for he possessed all beneath the surface. As with the souls that crossed into his dominion, the treasures of the earth belonged to him not by conquest, but by cosmic right.

Crown of Shadow

Among the sacred weapons forged in the fires of the Titanomachy, none aligned more perfectly with its bearer than the gift bestowed upon Hades. While Zeus received the thunderbolt and Poseidon claimed the trident, Hades was granted a relic not of noise or spectacle—but of silence. Forged by the Cyclopes, the Helm of Darkness was a powerful weapon, granting invisibility even before the gaze of gods.

With this celestial vestige, Hades moved like death itself—unseen, inevitable, and unstoppable. It allowed him to slip through enemy lines without a whisper, to pass unseen through the fabric of war, and to strike before his foes even knew he was near. The helm was more than a weapon. It was a symbol of Hades' essence. Unlike his emotional brothers, his was the quiet power, the unseen force that governed from beneath the world, where fear and fate met in silence.

In the clash between gods and Titans, the Crown of Shadow proved invaluable. While Zeus scorched the skies and Poseidon shattered mountains, Hades crept into the Titans' strongholds, unseen and unchallenged, unraveling their power from within. The hidden one was the unseen blade of the divine war—no less vital, and all the more terrifying for it.

Long after the war had ended, the helm remained one of the most revered artifacts in all mythology. It was given only in times of dire need. To Perseus, who used it to evade the gaze of Medusa. To Hermes, who donned it for missions cloaked in secrecy. Yet always, it returned to its true master, the silent sovereign of the dead, whose power lay not in spectacle, but in respect.

A Throne Apart

Though born of Cronus and counted among the Olympians, Hades stood apart. His throne was not set upon the heights of Olympus but deep within the shadowed heart of the earth. Hades' domain was fixed beneath all things—unchallenged, yet forever confined. His power was absolute, but it was bound to the dead. He did not govern the living, he awaited their departed souls.

This distinction made Hades formidable, but not omnipotent. His strength lay not in spectacle, but in certainty—his rule not loud, but eternal. The skies may rage, the seas may roar, but death does not falter. Hades ensured that no soul escaped its destined end, and even the gods, immortal though they were, respected his authority over the spirits of the dead.

Yet even the lord below was not untouched by the laws of balance. In time, his realm found its queen—Persephone—whose arrival would bind the worlds above and below in the rhythm of loss and return.

Perhaps the clearest sign of his separation was found in his solitude. Unlike Zeus or Poseidon, who moved freely among mortals or mingled with other gods, Hades rarely left his realm. His appearances upon Olympus were rare and met with unease, for he carried with him the weight of finality. His power did not inspire festivals or love—it inspired silence. The King of Shadows was not adored, but he was honored, for his was the kind of power no one could outrun.

Yet in that isolation, there was no weakness. Hades reigned over the one realm that all would enter. He was the keeper of the dead, the warden of hidden wealth, and the final authority in the cosmic order. Hades governed the one truth that none could escape—life's final certainty. In that, his power was unmatched.

SYMBOL OF THE AFTERLIFE

Feared by mortals, revered by priests, and often misunderstood by poets, Hades holds a distinct place in Greek mythology. One shaped not by spectacle, but by silence and inevitability. His myths reveal a god who governs the boundary between life and death with solemn authority, appearing rarely yet powerfully in the stories of gods and mortals alike. Unlike his brothers, Hades inspired few temples, yet his presence permeated rituals, funerary rites, and art alike. He was not worshiped to gain favor but acknowledged to maintain balance. Imagine ruling forever yet unseen; hearing prayers spoken in fear, not faith. From ancient vase paintings to modern visions of the afterlife, his shadow endures, a sovereign whose silence still defines how we imagine death, judgment, and what lies beyond.

> *"There is no man who can escape his fate,*
> *not even if he is descended from the gods."*
> — Homer, *Iliad*

Seed of the Underworld

Of all the myths that shaped the Greek understanding of life, death, and divine order, none endures more deeply—or reveals Hades more fully—than the tale of Persephone. It is a story of longing and consequence, of balance and transformation, explaining both the sorrowful change of seasons and the shared sovereignty of the Underworld. In its telling, Hades becomes not merely the lord of the dead, but a catalyst in the eternal cycle of loss and renewal.

Persephone, daughter of Demeter and goddess of spring's joy, lived untouched by grief in meadows blooming with wildflowers. She was innocence incarnate, radiant and free beneath the sun. But Hades, watching from below, saw in her not only beauty but a presence that could match his own, a dark consort to stand with him on the throne. The king of the Underworld had no queen, no companion, and in Persephone, he beheld the one who could complete his dominion.

One fateful day, lured by the sight of a narcissus, a flower sacred to the Underworld, Persephone reached for its bloom. At that moment, the earth shuddered, and a great chasm tore open the soil. From its depths thundered Hades in his black chariot, drawn by immortal steeds. In a single motion, he seized her and vanished back into the Underworld, the earth sealing above them as if untouched by divine upheaval.

Demeter's grief soon turned to celestial wrath. Abandoning her role as goddess of the harvest, she cast the world into famine. Crops failed, rivers dried, and mortals cried out for mercy. At last, Zeus—who had known of Hades' intent—could remain silent no longer. The King of Olympus sent Hermes to retrieve Persephone, but by the time the messenger reached her, she had eaten a single pomegranate seed—food of the dead. Bound now to the Underworld, she could not return in full. A pact was forged where Persephone would spend part of the year above with her mother, and part below as Queen of the Dead.

Thus began the eternal rhythm of the seasons. When Persephone rises, Demeter rejoices, and the world blooms anew. When she descends, the earth mourns, and winter falls. In this myth, Hades is not cast as villain but as transformation embodied—a force of passage, not destruction. The twilight realm is not an end, but a turning point. Through Persephone, the Underworld was shown to be a transformation, where loss becomes renewal, and death itself becomes the seed of life.

A Distant Brother

Among the radiant figures of Mount Olympus, Hades stood apart. An Olympian by birth, but not by presence. While his siblings quarreled, conspired, and mingled freely with mortals, Hades remained distant, rooted in the twilight of his silent kingdom. He had little interest in the passions of the living or the petty rivalries of his kin. His world lay beneath all things, untouched by mortal chaos and divine whim. When he did emerge, the air itself changed. Time seemed to still, and eternity looked back. His arrival was a mirror held to the face of eternity. A reminder that even the gods could not outrun fate.

One of the rare moments he walks among them appears in *The Iliad*, when Heracles, in a feat of defiance, wounded Hades with an arrow. Forced to ascend from the Underworld, the god of the dead sought healing upon Olympus. In that moment, the immortals glimpsed a truth often forgotten—that even Hades could bleed. He was not beyond pain, only beyond reach.

Yet even in absence, his presence loomed. In times of cosmic upheaval, such as the war against the Giants, the gods did not dare overlook him. Hades, unseen and unyielding, remained a force none could ignore. His dominion was not temporal, but eternal. To defy him was to invite not death, but something far worse. The unending silence in the abyss of Tartarus, where even gods feared to descend. The master of the hidden kingdom did not need to walk among them to be remembered. His power was not in voice or spectacle. It was in the stillness that binds all things to fate.

Gods of the Departed

The Greeks were not alone in envisioning a realm beyond death, nor was Hades the only deity to preside over such a place. Across the ancient world, gods and goddesses ruled the dead, each reflecting their civilization's vision of what lies beyond the final breath. And yet, when placed beside figures such as Ereshkigal of Mesopotamian myth or Hel of Norse legend, Hades stands apart— not in cruelty or chaos, but in restraint and order.

Ereshkigal, Queen of the Mesopotamian Underworld, governed a dominion steeped in sorrow. The souls who entered her realm were stripped of light and joy, condemned to a joyless shadow without reprieve. Her rule was absolute, but bleak—her domain, a mirror of despair. Unlike Hades, who ensured the dead found their proper place within a structured and balanced order, Ereshkigal's kingdom offered no such justice—only the fate of decay.

Hel, daughter of Loki and ruler of the Norse dead, commanded a land not unlike Hades in structure but colder in spirit. Her domain welcomed those who had not perished in glory, the ordinary souls, unmarked by fame or flame. Where Hel reigned with chill indifference, Hades governed with solemn purpose and law. The King of the Dead was not a throne of apathy, but of necessity. Hades was not a god of death alone, but of transition, ensuring that all souls passed where they must, bound by law, not whim. In this, Hades was a guardian of balance, a silent force who held the boundary between worlds.

Eternal Shadow

Across centuries of art and storytelling, Hades has worn many faces—some reverent, others distorted. In ancient Greek pottery, he was often rendered as a solemn figure, seated in stillness upon his obsidian throne, with Persephone at his side. Unlike Zeus, cast mid-thunderbolt, or Poseidon with his churning seas, Hades was depicted in perfect repose—watchful, unmoved, and unshaken. His power required no spectacle, his authority no display, for death itself was his proof.

As cultures evolved, so too did his image. The Romans named him Pluto, binding him more to the wealth beneath the earth than to the dead within it. Over time, medieval Christian thought blurred his identity with that of the Devil, a comparison born of misunderstanding. Hades ruled no fiery pit, nor did he delight in suffering. He was not a tempter or rebel, but a custodian of order in a cosmos that demanded boundaries between life and what comes after.

In modern retellings, his form has shifted once more. Films, novels, and games often recast him as a villain—ambitious and cunning, a dark mirror to Zeus. The most well-known of these is Disney's *Hercules*, where Hades appears as a fast-talking, flame-haired trickster, more mischief than majesty. While these portrayals entertain, they stray far from mythic truth. The Hades of old did not covet Olympus. He did not rage against his brothers. The Lord of the Underworld ruled without envy, distant yet dutiful, content within the silence of his realm.

Yet through every transformation, one thing remains. Hades endures as a figure of profound fascination. He is not Thanatos, the death-spirit who gently escorts souls across the veil. Hades is their keeper, their warden, and their final host. Neither hero nor villain, he is something rarer. A god who does not command love or fear, but balance. In a world ruled by chaos and ambition, Hades remains the still point in the turning sphere as the eternal sovereign of what awaits us all.

WHERE ALL PATHS LEAD

Of all the gods who shaped the ancient world, Hades remains the most enigmatic, a ruler not of thunder or tide, but of silence and law, of endings that sustain beginnings. Unlike his Olympian brothers, he sought neither glory nor dominion over the living. He ruled from the depths, distant yet essential, ensuring that the cycle of life and death turned unbroken. Feared by mortals and misunderstood by poets, Hades was no god of cruelty, but of consequence, a force of order that binds the mortal and divine alike. In his stillness, we glimpse our own — the silence that waits for all.

Yet even in his solemn reign, he did not dwell in darkness alone. Persephone, the Queen he claimed, and the goddess who chose to remain, brought transformation to his realm. Her presence wove light into shadow, turning death toward renewal and absence toward return. Through her, the Underworld itself became a mirror of the living world above. A place of endings, but also of promise.

As the stillness of Hades yields to the stirrings of her descent and rise, we follow Persephone into the mysteries of passage—the turning of the seasons, the union of earth and the veil, and the eternal rhythm through which all things die, and live again.

CHAPTER 2

PERSEPHONE

Queen of Spring and Shadow

The tale of Persephone's abduction stands as one of the most enduring myths in Greek tradition, a narrative where divine will, mortal grief, and cosmic order converge. With Zeus granting silent consent, Hades rose from the depths to claim Persephone, shattering her innocence and setting the cycle of life and death into motion. Her descent into the Underworld marked not only the loss of spring's joy, but the awakening of her true power, bound by shadow yet never broken. She emerged reborn—part queen, part maiden, ruler of the dead and herald of renewal. Her journey, repeated with the turning of the year, became the hallowed continuum of the seasons, forever entwining her destiny with the world above and below.

> *"And he seized her against her will,*
> *put her on his golden chariot,*
> *And drove away as she wept.*
> *She cried with a piercing voice,*
> *Calling upon her father, the son of Kronos,*
> *who is the highest of all."*
> — *Homeric Hymn to Demeter*

The Silent Pact

Persephone's story does not begin in darkness, but beneath the bright vault of Olympus, where fate was quietly decided. Hades, the solemn king of the Underworld, yearned for a queen, not for pleasure or conquest, but for companionship in his silent dominion. His gaze fell upon Persephone, daughter of Demeter and Zeus, a maiden of spring, untouched by sorrow, radiant with life. She was everything his kingdom was not—warmth to his silence, bloom to his stillness. Yet in the kingdom below, love does not bloom by courtship, and destiny moves not through romance, but certainty. Hades turned to Zeus, seeking consent to claim the maiden as his bride.

Zeus, ever entangled in celestial politics and private schemes, granted his approval. He saw in the union no disorder, only harmony—life joined with death, spring bound to silence. But he knew Demeter, Persephone's mother, would never allow such a union. Fiercely protective, the goddess of the harvest saw her daughter as a spirit of the living world, one who must never be touched by the dominion of the dead. So Zeus, in his cunning, withheld the truth. He gave Hades permission, but no guidance, turning his gaze elsewhere as the course of fate unfurled.

And so the trap was set. One quiet day, as Persephone wandered a sunlit field far from her mother's watch, she was drawn to a narcissus of otherworldly beauty, a flower sacred to the dead. As her hand reached toward it, the ground trembled and tore open. From the depths thundered Hades in his chariot, drawn by black horses wreathed in flame and mist. In a flash, he rose from the earth, seized the maiden, and vanished beneath the soil. The scent of crushed narcissus lingered long after the earth closed above her. The field was stilled. The earth stood quiet. For a moment, the world above did not yet know what had been taken. And from that moment, the living and the dead would never again stand apart.

Turning of the Seasons

When Demeter discovered Persephone's disappearance, her grief thundered through the mortal world. She wandered the earth in anguish, crying out her daughter's name, but no voice returned from the depths. What began as sorrow soon flared into divine wrath, for Persephone was not merely a daughter, but the heart of the harvest, and her loss tore the sacred bond between mother and earth. When Demeter learned the truth, that Hades had taken Persephone into the Underworld, her rage darkened the sky.

In her mourning, Demeter withdrew from her godly duties. The fields withered. Seeds slept beneath the soil. The soil grew cold, and famine spread across the land. Mortals, starving and desperate, lifted their prayers to Olympus. But Zeus, bound by his complicity, hesitated. He had granted Hades permission, cloaked in secrecy, and now the harmony of the world trembled beneath the weight of that decision.

At last, Zeus acted. He sent Hermes, fleet-footed herald of the gods, into the Underworld to retrieve the lost maiden. Hades, bound by law but unwilling to surrender the queen he had come to cherish, offered Persephone a single pomegranate seed, a gesture both tender and cunning. She ate the seed, unaware of the ancient law. To taste the food of the dead is to bind oneself to the Underworld forever.

When Hermes led her back into the world above, the truth was revealed. Persephone could not remain. Her fate now straddled two worlds. A compromise was struck, one that would shape the turning of time itself. She would spend part of the year in the Underworld with Hades, and part with Demeter in the land of the living.

And thus, the seasons began their endless turn. When Persephone rises, Demeter rejoices and the world bursts into bloom—spring and summer flourish in celebration. But when Persephone returns to the twilight, her mother grieves, and the land retreats into silence. Autumn falls. Winter reigns. In Persephone's circle of descent and return, the Greeks found not just an explanation for the changing seasons, but a mythic cadence echoing the lasting truths of death, rebirth, and the enduring bond between love and loss.

Balance in the Veil

Persephone's abduction was not an end, but a metamorphosis. No longer just the daughter of Demeter, she emerged as something far more profound. A goddess who moved between two worlds. In her travel between light and dark, Persephone became the embodiment of duality—spring's bloom and winter's hush, maiden and queen, life and silence intertwined. She stood as a living reminder that the path to power often begins in loss, and that life and death are not opposites, but reflections of the same divine order.

In the Underworld, Persephone did not linger as a captive. She ruled alongside Hades, not as a shadowed consort, but as a ruler in her own right. Her presence softened the land of the dead—grace where once there was only silence. She guided souls with compassion, and offering comfort where once only darkness reigned. Her dual nature brought equilibrium to Hades' stern governance—where he enforced law, she extended understanding.

Above, she remained a goddess of fertility and rebirth. With each return to the surface, she brought with her the promise of renewal. The earth responded to her presence; flowers bloomed, fields awakened, and the frost of grief gave way to joy. She was not merely a goddess who came and went—she was the rhythm of life itself, the pulse of seasons, the breath of the earth. In Persephone, the Greeks saw both the unavoidability of death and the hope that follows.

Her myth became the foundation of the Eleusinian Mysteries, the most sacred rites of ancient Greece. In these secret ceremonies, initiates sought a deeper understanding of the afterlife and communion with the divine. Persephone was their guide, the one who had crossed the veil and returned, bearing wisdom from both worlds. In her, they placed their hope for a blessed fate beyond death, not through conquest, but through transformation.

Persephone's story is one of passage—of sorrow and return, of loss and rebirth. She is the bloom that survives the frost, the queen who rises from darkness, and the thread that binds the living to the dead. Through her, the Greeks found not only a symbol of seasonal change, but a mythic mirror for the soul's journey. She is balance incarnate—the still point between love and loss, fear and faith, ending and beginning. And in her timeless rhythm, they saw that even in the coldest shadow, life waits to rise again.

GODDESS BETWEEN WORLDS

Persephone's reign in the Underworld is the very embodiment of sacred order—a presence suspended between renewal and decay, mercy and law, mortality and divinity. No longer merely the daughter of Demeter, she now rules as Queen beside Hades, not in shadow, but in power. Her transformation from maiden to monarch endowed her with a rare and profound authority, to offer comfort to the souls of the dead while also upholding the continuum that governs them. She is the voice that softens judgment, the hand that holds the threshold between worlds—

guardian, sovereign, and symbol of the truth that death is not an end, but a return within the greater order.

> *"There, apart from all the gods,*
> *dread Persephone dwells,*
> *in her halls of shadow,*
> *ruling over the souls of the departed."*
> — Homeric Hymn to Demeter

Two Thrones

Persephone entered the Underworld as a maiden taken by force, but in time, she was transformed—not into a prisoner, but into a queen. The girl who once danced through sunlit meadows now sat upon a throne of black stone, cloaked in dignity and divine authority. She did not fade into the shadows of Hades' realm, nor was she content to linger in his wake. As Queen of the Dead, Persephone ruled with poise and purpose, a guardian of balance who carried the weight of judgment, grace, and inevitability.

Among the Olympians, theirs was a rare partnership. While Zeus ruled from Olympus and Poseidon from the sea—each with unquestioned autonomy—Hades ruled beside Persephone. Her presence brought harmony to the Underworld—tempering its severity with insight and grace. She was not merely a consort, but a sovereign in her own right—wise, commanding, and revered. In myth, she is described not only as gracious but as formidable, her authority unmistakable, her influence woven into the laws of the dead.

Every soul passed through her domain, from kings to commoners, heroes to forgotten names. And in each corridor of the Underworld—in Asphodel, Elysium, and Tartarus alike—her presence was felt. It was she who ensured that souls found their rightful place. Her rule, like her nature, balanced light and shadow. Where Hades upheld law, Persephone embodied mercy. Where death drew boundaries, she reminded the cosmos that even in stillness, there is grace. Together, they shaped a kingdom not of fear, but of order and remembrance—a dominion of cosmic passage.

Comforter of Souls

Where Hades stood as the unyielding warden of death, Persephone brought grace to the kingdom below. She was not only a queen, but a gentle hand in a kingdom of silence—a goddess who listened where others judged. In her stillness lay mercy.

In the Underworld, she was the comforter of souls, the one who met fear not with punishment, but with understanding. Many myths speak of her compassion, revealing a divinity who saw the sorrow of mortals not as weakness, but as the final echo of life.

In the tale of Orpheus, it is Persephone who softens the silence. When the grief-stricken bard descended into the Underworld to retrieve Eurydice, it was his mournful song that stirred her heart. Moved by his longing, Persephone persuaded Hades to grant the impossible—a mortal's chance to reclaim the dead. Though the trial failed and Eurydice was lost once more, Persephone's intervention revealed her deep empathy and power to intercede where even death might yield.

More than a queen, Persephone was a bridge—a sacred threshold between the living and the dead. She guided souls to their rest not with dread, but with dignity. In her presence, the final passage became less fearsome, touched by the memory of spring and the hope of return. Through her, the Greeks envisioned an afterlife not ruled solely by law, but softened by compassion. Death, under her gaze, became not a forsaking, but a farewell—overseen by a goddess who had known the light, walked the dark, and understood the fragile balance of both.

Hope Beyond the Verdict

Though Hades reigned supreme over the Underworld, it was the three Judges of the Dead—Minos, Rhadamanthus, and Aeacus—who weighed the souls of mortals and passed verdict on their eternal fate. These judges, impartial and resolute, upheld the sacred laws of justice. Yet even in this solemn tribunal, Persephone's presence lingered—not as a lawgiver, but as a quiet voice of compassion. As Queen of the Dead, she held no gavel, yet her influence shaped the balance between judgment and mercy.

Unlike the judges, bound by the strictness of divine law, Persephone possessed a deeper insight, the understanding of mortality. Her dual nature—of life and death—granted her wisdom to see beyond deeds alone. She knew that choices were often shaped by suffering, ignorance, or fate. Myths speak of her gentle hand in the halls of judgment—softening sentences, tempering vengeance, and ensuring that justice did not forget mercy. Through her, the Underworld became not merely a place of consequence, but of reflection.

Persephone's role in judgment extended beyond verdicts and punishments. As the sacred figure of the Eleusinian Mysteries, she became a symbol of hope—that the soul's journey did not end in condemnation, but in transformation. She offered peace to those who honored her rites—reminding the faithful that death was not final, but a passage; that even in the stillness of the Underworld, renewal endured.

Rites of Descent and Renewal

In the Eleusinian Mysteries—ancient rites shrouded in secrecy yet revered across Greece—Persephone's most sacred legacy took form. Celebrated annually in Eleusis, these ceremonies honored her descent into the Underworld and her return to the light, transforming myth into ritual and sorrow into revelation. To the Greeks, her journey was no mere tale—it was a living allegory for the endless cycle of life, death, and rebirth.

Within these Mysteries, Persephone was worshipped alongside her mother, Demeter, as a goddess who held the keys to the soul's destiny. The rites promised more than remembrance—they offered hope. Initiates believed that through understanding Persephone's path, they might transcend the aimless fate of the Asphodel Meadows and reach a more blessed afterlife. Her movement between worlds became a symbol of transformation—the soul's potential to rise renewed, even after the darkness of death.

The influence of these rites spread far beyond Eleusis, shaping the spiritual imagination of ancient Greece. Persephone was not only Queen of the Underworld but also a guide between worlds—a bridge from despair to hope, from loss to renewal. Her myth taught that death was not annihilation, but passage; not silence, but change. She offered comfort to those who feared the end and inspired those who sought something beyond it.

Through the Eleusinian Mysteries, Persephone transcended myth to become sacred truth. Her story echoed the deepest turnings of existence; decay and return, grief and joy, descent and ascent. In her, the Greeks found not only the shadow of mortality, but the promise of meaning. She is the goddess of what lies beyond, and in the hearts of those who sought her, the lasting bloom of renewal endured.

Eternal Return

Persephone's presence in the Underworld was as layered as the myth that surrounds her. She ruled not only as Queen—cloaked in dignity and balance—but as comforter to the dead and beacon to the living. She softened the silence of the grave with compassion, bridged the veil between worlds, and guided the soul's final passage with wisdom born of both light and shadow. Her influence reached beyond the realm of the dead—shaping rites, rituals, and the deepest reflections of human mortality. In her myth, the ancient Greeks saw not just a tale, but a sacred truth that life moves in cycles, and death is part of its divine design.

Persephone's story is one of becoming. From maiden to monarch, from spring's bloom to winter's hush, she reflects the continuum of existence itself. Her descent and return mirror the journey of every soul—into loss, into silence, and then, into light. She is a symbol of transformation, a goddess of everlasting renewal, and a promise that even the darkest path may lead once more to life. Through her, the Greeks found courage in the face of death, and in every ending, the whisper of a beginning yet to come.

WHERE DEATH BECOMES SPRING

Persephone's myth is the breath between worlds—the stillness before bloom, the shadow before light. She embodies the sacred harmony between death and renewal. Her dual existence binds her to the silence of the grave and the awakening of the earth, making her a living symbol of the eternal cycle. In her, the Greeks saw not contradiction, but harmony, life and death not as enemies, but as reflections of a deeper rhythm. Through Persephone, they understood that every descent holds the promise of return, and from every ending, something new must rise.

"But when the earth blooms with fragrant flowers of spring,
Then from the realm of darkness she rises again,
A light for gods and mortal men alike."
— *Orphic Hymn to Persephone*

Wither and Bloom

To the ancient Greeks, Persephone was more than the bride of Hades—she was the pulse of nature itself, the embodiment of the sacred wheel that binds life to death and death to rebirth. Though she rules in the Underworld, her spirit was rooted in the fertile soil of the earth above. In her descent each autumn, and her return each spring, the Greeks saw the rhythm of all living things, where dormancy gave way to bloom, and silence was merely the breath before awakening. She was the frost and the flower, the shadow and the renewal.

Her connection to fertility was inseparable from her bond with Demeter, her mother and counterpart. Together, they formed celestial harmony. Demeter as the steadfast nurturer, Persephone as the force of transformation. When Persephone descended into the Underworld, the earth grieved with Demeter—fields lay fallow, the harvest ceased, and nature held its breath. But with her return came resurrection; seeds stirred, blossoms awakened, and abundance returned to the land. In Persephone's journey, the Greeks found not only a myth of seasonal change but a sacred metaphor for life's impermanence and return.

Her myth offered both explanation and solace. It reminded the ancients that all life moves in revolutions—that decay is not an end, but a turning. To honor Persephone was to embrace the fragility of life and the promise that follows it. She was a goddess of fertility not for giving life, but for restoring it. In her, nature found its lifeforce, humanity found its mirror, and myth found its eternal bloom.

A Garden in the Shadow

What sets Persephone apart in the vast tapestry of Greek mythology is her unmatched duality. She is at once the dark consort and the harbinger of spring—an embodiment of opposites reconciled. Unlike Demeter, whose embodiment is bound to the fertile fields of the living, or Hades, whose dominion never leaves the shadows, Persephone dwells in both light and darkness. She moves between worlds not as a visitor, but as a sovereign of each.

In the Underworld, Persephone reigns with quiet power. She is the keeper of dignity among the dead, a presence that tempers the gloom of Hades' domain with poise and balance. Her rule is solemn, ensuring the laws are honored and the souls of the departed find their proper place. She brings grace to shadow, a reminder that death, too, deserves reverence. In her, the Underworld is transformed from a place of despair into a dominion of order, stillness, and consecrated finality.

Yet with the turning of the seasons, the maiden rises, bringing with her the pulse of life. Her return to the surface each spring awakens the slumbering earth, coaxing blossoms from barren ground and warmth from winter's chill. She is not merely a goddess who signals renewal. She is renewal itself. Her descent ensures the world's rest, her return its renewal. In this sacred turning, Persephone reveals the truth that life and death are not enemies, but lifelong companions in a single divine rotation.

To the ancient Greeks, she was more than myth—she was a symbol of resilience and return. A figure of sorrow and hope, loss and rebirth. Persephone reminded mortals that all things must fade, but through transformation, all things may rise again. Her story offered comfort in hardship and wisdom in grief, teaching that what dies may yet bloom, and what is taken may still return in time.

Whispers Through Eternity

Though the worship of the Olympian gods has faded into the echoes of time, Persephone's presence has never disappeared. Woven through sorrow and rebirth, her story rippled through the centuries—outlasting temples and ritual. More than myth, she became a symbol of balance, of transformation, and of the sacred truth that life and death are not opposites, but mirrors.

In later eras, Persephone's journey was reinterpreted through new spiritual lenses. Her descent into the Underworld and elevation to the world above bore striking parallels to Christian ideas of resurrection, redemption, and the soul's immortality. She became an archetype of hope, one who fell into darkness and rose again, carrying with her the promise of renewal. In this light, Persephone bridged ancient belief and evolving theology, shaping how later cultures perceived the boundary between the mortal and the eternal.

Her image endured not only in faith, but in art and imagination. From black-figure pottery to Renaissance masterpieces, Persephone was depicted as both maiden and monarch, her duality captured in brushstrokes and verse. Poets invoked her as a muse of mystery while philosophers saw in her myth a reflection of the soul's longing for understanding. Her story inspired those who sought meaning in life's fragility, and grace in its impermanence.

Even now, Persephone walks the halls of modern myth. She appears in novels, films, and illustrations, reimagined for new generations yet rooted in the same everlasting cycle. Her tale reminds us that within every shadow there may bloom a garden— that transformation is not an end, but a passage. She is Queen of the Dead, Bringer of Spring, and the sacred rhythm by which all things fall and rise anew.

QUEEN OF THE SACRED CYCLE

Persephone's place in the Greek cosmos was as layered as the shadows she ruled and as luminous as the light she carried. She led with dignity and grace, tempered judgment with mercy, and walked beside the dead not in shadow, but as a light within it. As Queen of the Underworld, she was not merely a consort, but a comforter, a guide, and a sovereign force who brought harmony to the chthonic realm. Her influence crossed the veil, shaping rituals, beliefs, and the hopes of the living. Through her story, the Greeks found meaning in the rotation of the seasons and the cycles of the soul, discovering in death itself the seed of return.

Her journey—from maiden to monarch, from spring's bloom to winter's hush—reflects the order that binds heaven and earth. In Persephone, we are reminded that darkness is not the end, but a passage; that even in descent, there is transformation. She reshaped the Underworld not with thunder or conquest, but through presence. Through her, the Underworld became more than a place of judgment—it became the axis upon which existence itself turns, where endings gave birth to beginnings and life stood forever in balance with death.

Yet the Underworld is more than the throne she shares with Hades. It is vast and veiled—a kingdom carved by rivers of memory and retribution, marked by gates and guardians, divided into lands of wandering, bliss, and despair. From the golden meadows of Elysium to the abyss of Tartarus, every soul's path mirrors the life it lived—and the justice it earned.

To glimpse the full measure of Persephone's dominion, we must descend into the world she governs—where the living do not tread, and the silence itself remembers. Beyond her throne lies a world vast and veiled, rivers that bind oaths, gates that guard memory, and lands where every soul meets its fate. There, in the shadowed heart of creation, the geography of eternity unfolds.

CHAPTER 3

LAND OF THE DEAD

![The Veins of Hades illustration]

The Veins of Hades

The Greek Underworld was no shapeless abyss, but a kingdom of sacred design—mysterious, immense, and ruled by ancient order. Winding through its gloom ran five primordial rivers, each carrying more than water. They bore memory, judgment, pain, and transformation. These rivers—Styx, Lethe, Acheron, Phlegethon, and Cocytus—were more than boundaries. They were living forces that shaped the soul's journey after death. They flowed like veins through the world below, binding all in silence and mist. In their names echoed the essence of the afterlife. Oath and fire, sorrow and forgetting, passage and fate. To cross them was to enter the mysteries of death itself, and to begin the soul's final descent. And first among these sacred waters flowed the Styx, the black Stream where even gods paused in silence, knowing that to name it was to summon its power.

> *"By that dread stream of oath, the black water of Styx, which even the blessed gods do fear to swear falsely."*
> — Homer, *Iliad*

Threshold of Shadow

Of all the rivers that flowed through the Greek Underworld, none carried greater dread or sanctity than the River Styx. It was more than a current of black water—it was the sacred boundary between the worlds of the living and the dead, the solemn threshold no soul could cross without transformation. To name the Styx was to summon its power. It surged with divine authority, feared by mortals and gods alike, its depths echoing with the finality of fate.

In myth, the river was personified by the Titaness Styx, who allied herself with Zeus during the war against the Titans. As a reward for her loyalty, Zeus honored her river with inviolable power. Any oath sworn upon the Styx became forever binding. Even the immortals trembled before this law. To break such a vow meant exile from Olympus and a year of voiceless shame. The Styx became the gods' ultimate seal, its waters the very blood of divine contract.

For mortals, the Styx marked the first step on the soul's final journey. At its bank waited Charon, the silent ferryman cloaked in shadow, demanding payment for passage. A coin—an obolos or danake—was placed beneath the tongue of the dead, ensuring their right to cross. But those buried without this offering were denied passage, left to drift along the mist-shrouded shores, lost and unheard. The Styx did not forgive the unprepared. Its toll was firm, its silence eternal. For in its current flowed the price of transition, the cost of being remembered—or forgotten.

Beyond the oath-bound waters, the current softens. From judgment's roar to oblivion's whisper, the soul drifts toward Lethe, the river that promises peace through forgetting.

Waters of Forgetfulness

Deeper within the Underworld's shadowed corridors flows a river more subtle, and more seductive, than the dread Styx. Lethe does not wound with fire or torment, it whispers, inviting the dead to drink and forget. Its name means "oblivion," and its current erases memory, identity, and all traces of the mortal life once lived. To drink from Lethe was to surrender everything—grief and joy, pain and love—until nothing remained but the empty hush of the soul.

In the teachings of the Orphic Mysteries, Lethe held a sacred function in the continuum of rebirth. Before a soul could return to the world of the living, it was said they must drink from Lethe's waters, wiping clean all memory of their former life. Yet the wise sought a different fate. Those who yearned to escape the wheel of reincarnation were counseled to find and drink from Mnemosyne, the river of memory, so they might retain the knowledge of their past and ascend beyond the mortal cycle. Lethe, then, became a river of choice; forget and begin again, or remember and transcend.

Lethe offered mercy, but also danger. In its gentle current was peace, the kind that comes from forgetting sorrow. But it also bore the risk of dissolving the self. For some, this oblivion was a blessing; for others, a betrayal. It was a river of rest and erasure, of stillness and surrender. And in its embrace, many souls vanished not into torment, but into silence.

Yet not all sought forgetting. Some were carried instead to Acheron, where memory clings like mist, and sorrow becomes the soul's only companion.

River of Woe

If the Styx marked the sacred boundary, Acheron was the mournful road that led within. Its name, drawn from ancient tongues, meant "woe" or "pain"—a river born not of rage or fire, but of sorrow. For many souls, Acheron was the first current they encountered on their descent, its black waters carrying the dead toward the deeper reaches of Hades' dominion. Where the Styx represented law and binding oaths, Acheron was burden, the weight of memory, regret, and unwept grief.

In some tellings, it was this river, not Styx, that Charon ferried his boat across, guiding the newly dead through its cold embrace.

Myth claimed the river was formed from the tears of the suffering, its waters infused with centuries of mourning. The Acheron was not a river of punishment, but of sorrow, a place where souls felt the full ache of what was lost, left unsaid, or undone in life. It was a current of reckoning, not judgment—a passage through pain, not beyond it.

Even among the living, the Acheron cast its shadow. In the rugged Epirus region of Greece, a real river bore its name, winding through bleak and misty landscapes. To the ancients, this was no ordinary stream. It was a threshold. They believed the veil between worlds thinned along its banks, and that to gaze upon its waters was to glimpse the path the soul would one day take. In myth and in earth, Acheron remained what it always had been, a river of sorrow that all must cross, where the echoes of life followed the dead into silence.

Beyond this mournful current, the air begins to tremble and burn—for here flows Phlegethon, the river of flame, where pain itself is made sacred.

Fire That Purifies

Where the other rivers of the Underworld whispered sorrow, silence, or forgetfulness, the River Phlegethon roared. Its name meant "flaming" or "blazing," and unlike its darker kin, its waters did not flow with darkness, but with fire. Phlegethon coursed with liquid flame, an unquenchable inferno that neither consumed nor waned. It wound its way through the deepest chasms of the Underworld, licking at the jagged edges of Tartarus, where the most cursed of souls were cast beyond salvation.

This river was the chosen crucible of divine punishment. It was here that the wicked, those who defied the gods or committed crimes too grievous to be forgiven, were hurled into the blaze. In Phlegethon's searing current, there was no mercy, only pain without end. It did not kill, for its purpose was not to destroy, but to punish. Phlegethon was a sentence, a flaming decree of cosmic justice that burned without respite.

And yet, not all saw it as vengeance alone. In Plato's philosophy, the river held another purpose, purification. Its flames, while fearsome, could cleanse the soul, scorching away the sins of former lives and preparing the spirit for rebirth. Whether viewed as torment or transformation, Phlegethon stood as a river of reckoning. It reminded the dead that in the Underworld, suffering was not without meaning, and that even in fire, there might flicker the hope of renewal.

Yet when the flames fade, only silence remains—and within that silence flows Cocytus, the river that remembers every cry.

Cry That Echoes Forever

Of all the rivers that wound through the Underworld, none was more sorrowful than Cocytus. Its very name meant "the river of wailing," and its waters were said to be fed by the endless tears of the damned. Along its fog-veiled banks wandered souls forsaken by fate. Those who had committed grave sins or died without proper rites— their lamentations rose in ceaseless agony. Where Lethe offered forgetfulness and Styx demanded passage, Cocytus offered only mourning, a soundless scream that echoed beyond time.

This was the river of the inconsolable, a place not of fire or judgment, but of unending despair. In later traditions, most famously in Dante's *Inferno*, Cocytus was reimagined not as a river but as a frozen lake at the deepest circle of Hell, its icy surface trapping traitors in mute, glacial torment. Here, betrayal was preserved in frost, not flame, and sorrow became stillness. Whether flowing or frozen, Cocytus symbolized the agony of separation—from the gods, from justice, from peace.

To the living, Cocytus stood as a dire warning. Those who defied divine law, denied the rites of death, or shattered sacred bonds risked this fate. Their cries would not be heard by the heavens, only by the dark water that mirrored their regret. Cocytus was the final river, the last echo in the Underworld—a lament that never ends, a sorrow too deep for silence.

Thus the five rivers converge—oath, oblivion, sorrow, flame, and lament—each a current in the vast anatomy of death, flowing together as the veins of the Underworld.

Veins of the Underworld

The rivers of the Underworld were more than waterways. They were veins of the afterlife, carrying the weight of judgment, memory, and transformation. Each flowed with its own truth—Styx with oath, Lethe with forgetting, Acheron with sorrowful passage, Phlegethon with purifying flame, and Cocytus with endless grief. Separately, they mirrored the fragments of the human soul—its regrets, its hopes, its sins, and its longing for peace. Together, they shaped a landscape not of chaos, but of order forged in shadow.

To cross them was to surrender to fate, to confront what life had left unresolved. In their currents, the Greeks saw not just punishment or reward, but meaning— the reckoning of the spirit with what it had been and what it might become. The rivers endured as symbols of that sacred journey, their names whispered across centuries as omens and echoes. In the Underworld, it was not the gates or the guardians that defined the path of the dead— it was the rivers that remembered, the rivers that ruled.

Yet beyond their converging currents, the land itself awaited judgment.

LANDS OF JUDGEMENT AND SHADOW

Beyond its rivers of sorrow and fire, the Underworld unfolded as a labyrinth of realms, each shaped by fate and each echoing the destiny of those who entered. It was a world not only of darkness, but of divine design, where punishment, reward, and silence coexisted. From the moment the dead passed through its gates, they began a journey across sacred terrain, through fields where the forgetful wandered, gardens where the virtuous found peace, and abysses where the damned endured eternal reckoning. These were not places of chaos, but of purpose, etched by the will of the gods, and haunted by the memory of life.

> "There stands a rock in the dreadful Underworld,
> Where the souls of the dead pass judgment,
> And the great chasms stretch deep into the gloom."
> — Homer, *Odyssey*

Gates of the Dead

Few mortals ever glimpsed the gates of the Underworld and returned to speak of them. Towering and impenetrable, they stood as the threshold between the sunlit world of the living and the silent dominion of the dead. Wreathed in shadow and solemn air, they marked the point of no return, a place where breath ceased, time unraveled, and the soul stepped beyond the veil. At their base loomed Cerberus, the monstrous hound of Hades, his three heads ever watchful. He was a sentinel of death's order, ensuring no living soul entered unbidden, and none of the dead escaped their fate.

The road to the gates was a desolate stretch of darkened terrain, stripped of warmth and memory. Beyond, the dead passed into the domain of Hades and the long journey toward judgment. Yet in myth, a rare few breached this sacred boundary. Orpheus, armed only with grief and song, stirred the hearts of the deathless and was granted passage. Heracles, driven by fate and might, tore through the gate itself to seize Cerberus as part of his Twelve Labors. These stories stand not just as feats of courage, but as reminders that even in a world ruled by finality, there are those who dared to cross the boundary between life and death.

The Meadows of Asphodel

Beyond the gates of the Underworld stretched the Asphodel Meadows, a land untouched by joy or torment, reserved for those whose lives were marked neither by heroism nor by shame. Here wandered the multitude. The farmers, artisans, merchants, and forgotten names. Neither unworthy nor wicked, their fate was not punishment but permanence. A quiet, lingering shadow of existence. The meadows were vast and still, veiled beneath an ashen sky, and carpeted in pale, ghostly asphodels—the flower of the dead, swaying in a wind that no longer belonged to the world above.

The spirits who dwelled in Asphodel were echoes of their former selves Memory faded, names dissolved, and purpose unraveled into silence. Unlike the blessed of Elysium who rejoiced, or the condemned of Tartarus who suffered, those in Asphodel simply were—drifting, whispering, half-remembering the light they once knew. It was not a place of cruelty, but of absence. A land of gray eternity, where ambition, sorrow, and ecstasy alike had been surrendered to the stillness of death. In Asphodel, the reward was rest, but never rebirth.

Fields of Eternal Spring

For the rare and righteous, those whose lives burned with extraordinary valor, wisdom, or divine favor, there awaited a paradise beyond shadows, the Elysian Fields. Unlike the dim meadows of Asphodel or the burning torments of Tartarus, Elysium shimmered with golden light and everlasting spring. Soft breezes stirred the air, music echoed without end, and the blessed walked freely among fields untouched by grief or time. Here, heroes, poets, and rulers feasted without hunger, danced without weariness, their joy untouched by sorrow.

Entry into Elysium was not won through mere piety or fortune. It was a reward reserved for the few who lived with uncommon virtue or who served the gods with unwavering devotion. In some traditions, Elysium lay at the farthest edge of the world, across the Western Sea, on the Isles of the Blessed, a land where death had no place. It was the Underworld's highest honor, its rarest grace.

Yet even paradise held its mysteries. According to the Orphic and Pythagorean traditions, a soul who reached Elysium could choose to return to life and walk the mortal path once more. If that soul achieved Elysium in three successive lifetimes, it was said they would ascend beyond mortality, becoming one with the divine and escaping the cycle of death and rebirth forever. In this, the

Elysian Fields were more than reward—they were a threshold to transcendence.

Throne of Silence and Stone

At the heart of the Underworld, deep beneath the trembling roots of the earth, rose the shadowed Palace of Hades. Rarely described in the ancient texts, yet always implied, it stood as the sovereign seat of the dead, a place not built for splendor, but for rule. Its towering halls, carved from obsidian and veined with precious gems torn from the Underworld's womb, gleamed faintly in the lasting dusk. It was a palace without celebration, a citadel of judgment, stillness, and law.

Unlike the radiant courts of Olympus, the palace of Hades held no feasts, no laughter, no revels echoing into the sky. It radiated the quiet authority of the inevitable—grim, absolute, and just. Within its great chamber, Hades controlled not with rage or ambition, but with solemn command. For part of the year, Persephone sat beside him, her presence softening the gloom, lending grace and renewal to a place otherwise steeped in silence.

Here, the Judges of the Dead—Minos, Rhadamanthus, and Aeacus—rendered their verdicts. Within these walls, souls were weighed, and their destinies assigned to Elysium's joy, Asphodel's neutrality, or Tartarus' torment. And from these halls also moved the Furies, winged agents of vengeance and justice, ensuring that no oath sworn upon the Styx went unpunished, and no sin escaped the notice of the dead.

This palace was not a prison, but a reckoning. It was the dark mirror of Olympus, and the fixed axis of mortal consequence. Feared by the living, revered by the gods, it stood as a monument to balance, a throne not forged by desire, but by necessity. For in the end, all paths led here, and in its silent halls, every soul was seen.

Where All Paths are Weighed

Before any soul could enter Elysium's light, Asphodel's stillness, or Tartarus' abyss, it first passed through the Antechamber of Judgment—a vast, hushed hall beneath the earth where the newly dead lingered in silence. Stripped of flesh, status, and name, the spirit stood bare before the laws of the gods. This was not a place of torment or welcome, but of reckoning, where time no longer moved, and only truth remained.

At the far end of the chamber, three thrones loomed beneath the vault of shadow. Here sat Minos, the final arbiter; Rhadamanthus, keeper of justice; and Aeacus, guardian of oaths. Brought here by Hermes Psychopompos, the silent guide of the dead, each soul stepped forth to be weighed beneath the gaze of eternity. There were no appeals nor illusions, only the measure of a life lived and the hallowed sentence it had earned.

Some souls stood unshaken, their deeds noble, their hearts pure, destined for Elysium's golden fields. Others bowed in fear, their crimes dragging them toward Tartarus and its torments. Most awaited no glory or damnation, but drifted quietly into Asphodel, forgotten by history yet spared from ruin. In this hall, the soul's path was revealed—not by favor, but by fate.

The Underworld laid bare its eternal truth. It was not a dominion of punishment, but of balance, a sacred mechanism by which every mortal, king or servant, poet or thief, must one day pass. No crown or prayer could alter the verdict. In the chamber, justice was not blind—it was absolute.

The Realm Beyond the Living

The Underworld was more than a land of the dead. It was a kingdom of memory, judgment, and fate. Beneath its shadows flowed the laws that bound all mortals, and even the gods honored its authority. It was here that every soul—hero or wanderer, poet or peasant—was given a final path. Some found glory in the golden fields of Elysium, others drifted in the gray silence of Asphodel, while the accursed suffered in the depths of Tartarus. Yet none were lost, each was weighed, judged, and remembered by the final realm that forgets no one.

It was a world ruled not by cruelty, but by equilibrium—a mirror of mortal consequence where oaths echoed and the soul's truth stood bare before divine law. The Greeks did not envision the Underworld as endless torment, but as the inevitable continuation of the mortal path, a place where final meaning was found, and the cycle closed in solemn majesty.

Though feared, it was not cursed. It was sacred. It was the end all must face, and the ground upon which myths of judgment, redemption, and rebirth were sown. In this land beyond the living, the dead found not oblivion, but their destined place in eternity.

THE DARKEST DEPTHS

Beyond the banks of the River Styx, past the silent meadows of the forgotten and the shadowed halls of judgment, there lay a place so dreadful, so utterly bereft of hope, that even the gods spoke of it in hushed tones. This was Tartarus—the abyss beneath all realms, a pit not merely of exile, but of divine retribution. It was the prison of the Titans, the graveyard of cosmic rebellion, and the final sentence for those whose crimes defied mortal comprehension.

Unlike Elysium, where the honored rejoiced, or Asphodel, where the ordinary drifted in gray repose, Tartarus was suffering made to never end. Here, darkness was not absence, but presence, a force alive and devouring, where time fractured and justice descended like flame. It was not merely death's dominion—it was punishment incarnate, the black heart of the Underworld itself.

> *"As far beneath the earth as heaven is above,*
> *there lies the dark and dreadful pit of Tartarus,*
> *wrapped in mist and guarded by unyielding gates."*
> — Hesiod, *Theogony*

Abyss of the Damned

Tartarus was no cave, no corner of Hades' realm—it was a cosmic chasm, far deeper than the Underworld itself, a void so far beneath the palace of the dead that a falling anvil would plummet for nine days before striking its floor. It was the final prison of defiance and desecration, sealed in silence, fear, and eternal flame. Even the Olympian gods, who had hurled the Titans into its depths, dared not draw near its threshold. Here lay the souls who had not merely sinned but had violated the celestial order. Those whose crimes fractured the cosmos or dared to mock the gods themselves.

Within this abyss rotted the most infamous figures in myth. Sisyphus, who cheated death, was cursed to endless labor, straining to roll a boulder uphill, only to watch it fall each time he neared the summit. Tantalus, who fed his son to the gods, stood forever thirsty and hungry, water and fruit always just out of reach. Ixion, who betrayed Zeus's sacred hospitality, was lashed to a flaming wheel, spinning without end. And the Danaids, fifty sisters who slew their husbands on their wedding night, were doomed to fill a leaky basin with water that would never rise. In Tartarus, punishment was not merely inflicted—it was designed, tailored to echo the soul's transgression for eternity. The gods did not forget, and in this deepest darkness, justice did not sleep.

Fall of the First Gods

Before mortal sinners ever trembled beneath Tartarus' curse, the abyss served a more ancient purpose as the prison of the Titans. These primordial deities, who once held rule over the cosmos, were overthrown in the cataclysmic war known as the Titanomachy. For ten years, the heavens burned as Olympians and Titans warred across sky and earth. When the final thunderbolt fell, Zeus stood victorious. To ensure their power would never rise again, the Titans were cast into Tartarus, bound in chains forged by Hephaestus and buried beneath the weight of fate itself.

Among these fallen immortals was Cronus, father of Zeus, Poseidon, and Hades. The same god who had swallowed his children in a vain attempt to alter prophecy. His downfall came not by fate, but by the very son he sought to destroy. Some later tales offer him redemption, claiming he was freed to rule over the Isles of the Blessed. But in older and darker myths, he remains bound in Tartarus, silent and brooding in defeat. Imprisoned beside him were his monstrous allies and enemies alike, the Hecatoncheires, beings of overwhelming force, once shackled by the Titans but now serving as their jailers in turn.

Their punishment in Tartarus was more than justice. It was a monument to the authority of Olympus. The Titans had controlled the cosmos, but defied the new order, and for that, they were banished to a depth beyond gods and mortals alike. Their chains were not merely of metal, but of meaning. Tartarus became not only a prison, but a warning that no power, however great, could stand against the will of Zeus or the balance of the divine. It was the grave of forgotten reigns and a place where even gods could fall.

Shadow Beyond Punishment

Tartarus was the abyss of justice, but deeper still, hidden beneath even the reach of godly chains, lay a domain spoken of only in whispers, the nightmare beneath the Underworld. It was not a prison, but a place of distortion, where souls were not merely punished but unmade. Rarely named in myth and scarcely understood, this domain existed beyond law and beyond hope, a final exile for the truly irredeemable, where torment was no longer physical, but existential.

Here, the damned did not suffer as themselves. They became something else. Souls steeped in evil were consumed by their own corruption, transformed into monstrous shades, creatures whose forms bore the shape of their crimes. The air reeked of guilt and dread. Shadows moved not as reflections, but as hunters. Time fractured. Whispers filled the void, murmuring sins that could never be undone. This was no world of judgment. It was a mirror of what the soul had chosen to become.

Some ancient retellings place Tartarus under the watch of Nyx, the primordial Night, before whose presence even Zeus shuddered. Her children, Thanatos, the quiet death; Hypnos, the bringer of sleep; and the Oneiroi, bearers of dreams and nightmares, moved between this realm and the waking world. Others claimed this blackened region belonged to the Furies, who tore into the spirits of the unatoned, their vengeance unrelenting and beyond appeal.

But perhaps the most terrible truth was this. For some, Tartarus was not the end, but a threshold. There were souls so foul that even the torments of chains and flame could not contain them. These were cast into the Realm of Nightmares, where their punishments became illusions made real, hallucinations turned endless. Here, the dead did not merely remember their worst deeds—they relived them endlessly, shattered by regret, undone by the weight of what they had been. It was a place where the soul was not broken, but devoured.

Beyond Mercy

To the ancient Greeks, Tartarus was not merely a place of torment, but the embodiment of consequence. It was where the scales of the cosmos tipped with finality, and where the heaviest debts of the soul were paid in unrelenting measures. To be condemned to Tartarus was not death. It was what followed when justice could no longer be delayed. The Olympian order, built on divine balance, demanded that every crime find its answer. In Tartarus, there was no appeal. Only eternity.

Yet even in this pit of finality, faint echoes of hope survived. Orphic traditions, steeped in mystery and spiritual renewal, whispered of purification and release. They spoke of cycles, of rebirth, and of a soul's long road back to the light. Though rare and uncertain, these beliefs offered a distant glimmer; that perhaps not all chains were forever, that some might one day rise from shadow, cleansed and restored. In these teachings, Tartarus became not just a punishment, but a crucible.

Still, for most, their fate was sealed. Tartarus and the nightmare realms beyond remained domains of endless exile, where Titans, traitors, and the soul-corrupted vanished into silence. It was a place not marked on maps, not spoken of in ritual—only felt in fear and remembered in myth. A land without dawn, where the echoes of wrongdoing outlasted the voices of the damned, and where mercy was a stranger. In the Greek imagination, it was the most terrible fate of all; not death, but abandonment.

BOUNDARIES OF SOULS

The Underworld was no shapeless abyss nor a blind chasm. It was a realm of precision, meaning, and divine law. Each of its landmarks, from the rivers that carved the soul's passage to the gates that sealed fate, served a sacred purpose. The meadows where the forgotten drifted, the golden fields of the blessed, and the abyss where the wicked were broken, all mirrored the ancient Greek understanding of life's resonance in death. Memory, judgment, fate, and redemption took form in geography, shaping a world that mirrored the soul's final reckoning.

Bound by unyielding laws and ruled by gods who enforced cosmic order, the Underworld offered not just punishment or reward. It offered placement. For many, it was a place of sorrow. For some, stillness. For the rarest few, transcendence. And yet through all its regions ran a deeper truth. The Underworld was not only an ending, but a passage unfading. It was the final chapter in the mortal story—the threshold of souls, where order yields to journey.

No soul could begin that journey without the ferryman. Charon, the silent guide, stood watch upon the shores of Styx. With oar in hand and shadow in his gaze, he ensured that none passed unbidden—and that none returned. Those buried without coin or rite remained stranded, nameless and unmoored. As we depart the still lands of the dead, we follow the figure who carried every soul across its first great threshold. In the next chapter, we meet Charon—the keeper of the crossing, and the herald of the end.

CHAPTER 4

CHARON

Ferryman of Souls

Though Hades ruled the Underworld and its laws echoed with divine authority, it was Charon, the silent ferryman, who bore the spirits of the dead across the black waters of the Styx. Cloaked in shadow and unmoved by prayer, he stood at the threshold of existence, demanding his fare, a single coin to cross the veil. Those properly buried passed into his boat. The rest drifted in mist, lost between realms. He was no judge, no tormentor, but the one all must face. Tireless and eternal, Charon rowed the last journey of every mortal.

> *"There is a port where all must come,*
> *Who dwell upon the earth;*
> *And one lone boatman waits to guide*
> *The silent throng across the tide."*
> — Virgil, *Aeneid*

Oarsman of the River Styx

Amid the twilight mists of the Underworld, where silence thickens and the shadows breathe with memory, moved a solitary figure both feared and respected. Charon, the ferryman of souls, was a spectral guardian of the River Styx, bound to its ill-fated waters by ancient law. Neither fully living nor entirely dead, he was a relic of the world's first breath, a being who predated kingdoms, who would endure until the final soul was summoned to rest. Shrouded in the stillness of eternity, his presence upon the river marked the departed's first step into the world of the dead.

He was often depicted as gaunt and skeletal, his hollow gaze fixed upon the horizon of no return. Charon spoke no words, for none were needed. He showed no cruelty, yet no mercy. His task was fixed in the order of the cosmos, to receive those who came with toll and rite, and to reject those unprepared. He was no servant, but an agent of necessity, ensuring that the living did not trespass, and that the dead found their rightful course. In his silence lay order itself.

The River Styx, which he alone traversed, was not water in any mortal sense. Its darkened current shimmered with sorrow, heavy with the weight of unspoken regrets and severed ties. Some said it held the power to erase the last vestiges of mortal being, severing the soul from memory and flesh alike. Others believed its waters carried the binding force of godly oath, honored even by Zeus himself. Whatever its truth, the ferryman's role upon the Styx was absolute. He was the threshold incarnate, the boatman none could bribe, outrun, or deceive.

Price to Cross the Veil

To cross the waters of the Styx and find rest beyond the veil, a soul required more than courage. It needed a toll. Typically, an obolos coin or danake, this humble token was placed in the mouth of the deceased, not as a mere funerary rite but as sacred currency. It was the fare owed to Charon, and without it, the dead were condemned to wander the mournful banks, nameless and unreceived, lost in the misted silence that clung to the river's edge. The payment was not tradition—it was law, woven into the very fabric of death's domain.

The origin of this offering spoke to a deeper truth that the journey to the Underworld was no ordinary transition. It was a sacred crossing, one that demanded reverence and readiness. The coin served not as a bribe but as an acknowledgment, a ritual sign that the soul had fulfilled its mortal course and now sought entrance to the next world. In this simple gesture, the Greeks affirmed the ordered cosmos they believed in, where even death followed divine design, and chaos was kept at bay through rite and obligation.

Yet the offering also drew a sharp line between those who had and those who had not. For the poor and unprepared, the price of passage could become an eternal burden. Some tales whispered that Charon, though unyielding, was not without discernment. On rare occasions, he might carry a soul of noble deed without payment, moved by destiny or pity. In rarer moments, gods intervened, allowing heroes like Heracles and Orpheus to pass freely, their presence sanctioned by powers even Charon could not defy.

Despite his grim silhouette and quiet manner, Charon was no torturer. He inflicted no judgment, delivered no pain. His was the duty of transport, not retribution. The final judgement awaited distant shores, in the shadowed halls where the Judges of the Dead held court. Charon's task was singular, eternal, and absolute. To carry those who had paid the sacred fare into the kingdom from which no mortal returns.

Yet not all who reached his shore found passage.

Shadows at the River Edge

For those who approached the River Styx without offering, the afterlife did not simply delay—it turned away. Denied passage by Charon, these forsaken souls lingered at the edge of death, caught between realms. They became shadows without destination, murmuring along the blackened shores, their presence a restless echo of lives unloved or rites unfulfilled. In that liminal space, where the river touched neither judgment nor peace, they drifted— unseen, unheard, unremembered.

Among the ancient Greeks, such a fate inspired dread deeper than death itself. Burial was not merely a ritual. It was the seal that allowed the soul to cross. Without it, the spirit was cast adrift, unable to enter the world beyond. These wandering dead, known as aoroi, were not silent in their misery. They were said to haunt the living, their cries clinging to the night like mist, demanding remembrance or revenge. Their mourning was not for life lost, but for their release to the afterlife denied.

In rare tales, redemption glimmered through the haze. A living kin, stirred by grief or guilt, might return to offer the sacred coin, placing it as tribute upon the departed's behalf. In other whispers, it was believed that a century of wandering might soften the laws of the Underworld, allowing even the unburied to pass at last. Yet what was one hundred years to a soul trapped in fog, nameless and alone. Such a span stretched like eternity, a punishment not of fire but of forgetting.

Charon, ever impassive, did not pause. His boat glided through the dark with unwavering rhythm, accepting only those who had honored the rites. He did not comfort the stranded nor alter his course. His silence was final. Behind him, the mist folded over the forsaken, and the river flowed on, its shores haunted by voices the living dared not hear.

Herald of the Final Shore

In the great cycle of life and death, Charon stood as an immutable presence, neither benevolent nor wrathful, but eternal.

He did not judge, punish, or reward. He simply was. As the ferryman of the dead, he upheld the sacred boundary that separated the world of the living from the kingdom of shadows, ensuring that every soul, once unmoored from breath, found its destined shore. Through him, the laws of the Underworld were honored, and the order of all things maintained.

Where Hades reigned with sovereignty over the realm beyond, Charon moved along its borders, the embodiment of passage itself. He was not the end, but the crossing. His myth carried with it the chill of inevitability—the quiet certainty that no life escaped his reach. His vessel, small and unadorned, glided across the Styx in endless rhythm, mirroring the heartbeat of mortality; steady, solemn, and ceaseless.

Charon waits still, upon the blackened shore, hand outstretched to receive his due. His boat rocks gently in the mist, its bow pointed toward eternity. And when the next soul arrives, cloaked in silence and shadow, he will row once more—unchanged, undeterred, the tireless herald of the world beyond.

THRESHOLD MADE FLESH

Charon stands as a silent pillar within Greek myth—unyielding, unspoken, and eternal. More than a ferryman, he is the threshold given form, a figure whose presence ensured the sanctity of passage from life to death. He appears not in speech, but in presence—in the shadows of heroes, in the laments of the unburied, and in the art of every age. His silence is not absence but law, his role not power, but order. Through him, the Underworld maintained its rhythm, and every soul, in time, found its place upon his boat.

> *"And there the aged boatman, Charon, grim and filthy,*
> *watches over the water, ferries the souls of the dead*
> *across the dark and dreadful current."*
> — Virgil, *Aeneid*

Heroes at the River Edge

Few among mortals dared to tread the path into the Underworld, and fewer still returned to speak of what they saw. Yet within the oldest lore, there are those whose fates led them to the edge of the River Styx, where Charon stood as sentinel between worlds. Heroes, mourners, seekers of truth. Each approached the ferryman with purpose, and in doing so, joined the rare fraternity of the living who beheld his shadow and survived.

Orpheus, the bard whose sorrow could silence gods, descended with nothing but his lyre and his broken heart. In pursuit of Eurydice, lost to the veil of death, he sang beneath the ashen sky. The melody he played was not one of defiance, but of grief so pure that even Charon, bound by the laws of death, paused in stillness. No toll passed between them. Only music. And so, the ferryman, unmoved by gold but swayed by lament, ferried Orpheus across the black waters toward Hades' throne.

Heracles, son of thunder and strength incarnate, faced Charon not with song but with unshakable will. Tasked with seizing Cerberus from the depths of the Underworld, he arrived not in mourning but in conquest. Charon, enforcer of sacred order, met a force beyond law. Though no soul alive should cross without the offering, Heracles bore godly sanction. The ferryman, unflinching even in the face of legend, yielded—not from fear, but from fate. But not all who faced the ferryman sought love or conquest.

Odysseus, the cunning wanderer, sought truth. Guided by Circe's enchantments, he stood upon the edge of the Underworld, summoning the dead to speak their wisdom. He did not ride the ferryman's boat, yet he stood near its moorings, close enough to feel the hush that lingers at the river's edge. There, in that liminal hush, he glimpsed the weight of death's passage, and the stillness that Charon guards.

Warden of the Crossing

Though legends speak of rare heroes who passed into the Underworld with music, strength, or divine favor, Charon himself remained steadfast. His vigil was eternal. Neither persuasion nor desperation could sway him. He was the enforcer of a single law. Only those who came prepared, bearing the fare for passage, would be ferried across the dark waters of the River Styx. His role was not to judge, but to guard the boundary, upholding the order decreed by the gods.

Charon could not be corrupted, yet mythology allows glimpses of moments when the sacred pattern bent, if only for the most exceptional. Orpheus, armed with grief and melody, softened the silence. Heracles, bearing divine command, defied the boundary. Odysseus, guided by rites and enchantment, came close enough to taste death's breath. But these were not mortal triumphs over Charon. They were sanctioned exceptions, granted by forces greater than even he. For all others, the ferryman's law remained absolute.

And so, for the uncounted souls who arrived without an offering, no music could move him. They lingered in the subtle fog, their voices hollow, their fate unsealed. Charon passed them by with unbroken rhythm, his boat cutting through the waters that knew no return. He did not scorn them—he simply obeyed. In his silence was a sacred weight. The boundary between the living and the dead was not his to question, only to guard.

Echoes of the Ferryman

The figure of Charon did not fade with the twilight of the Greek gods. Instead, he endured, drifting through the pages of history as a symbol of finality, liminality, and the inescapable passage between worlds. From classical poetry to Renaissance paintings and into modern minds, Charon's silhouette—silent, stern, and shrouded in shadow—remained a fixture in how humanity imagined death's crossing. He was more than myth; he became metaphor.

In Virgil's *Aeneid*, Charon appears with his ancient gravity intact. The Roman poet described him as old and powerful, with eyes like burning coal and a cloak stained by centuries. When Aeneas approached the Styx, bearing the golden bough that marked him for safe passage, Charon did not yield out of awe or pity. He scrutinized the hero like all others, waiting until celestial sanction compelled him. In this moment, as in all others, Charon did not decide. He obeyed. His role was to ensure that none passed who had not earned the right.

Artists, too, were drawn to Charon's solemn image. On ancient Greek pottery, he stands hunched at the prow, oar in hand, guiding shadows through still waters. Michelangelo later cast him as a wrathful force in *The Last Judgment*, while Delacroix painted him with ghostly dread and eternal fatigue. In Dante's *Inferno*, Charon reemerges as a demonic ferryman, cursing souls as he drives them toward punishment. Yet even in transformation, his essence persists—unyielding guide, herald of the final shore. His name lives on in celestial echoes, as the great moon Charon follows Pluto through the void, eternally bound to the god of the dead.

Watcher at the Crossing

Charon was never merely a spectral oarsman among the forgotten dead. He was the embodiment of transition, the keeper of the threshold between worlds. In Greek thought, he was not counted among the great legends, yet his presence was indispensable. Through his silent watch and relentless duty, the realms of life and death remained divided, each soul accounted for, each crossing earned. He reminded mortals that death was not chaos, but a passage with rites, tolls, and laws—an order that demanded reverence.

His shadow stretches far beyond the folklore and myths that birthed him. Charon's boat still glides through art, literature, and memory, cutting through the mystical, black waters of the Styx with quiet finality. He stood beside heroes, stared from ancient vases and vaulted ceilings, and whispered through the lines of poets and philosophers alike. In every retelling, he remains unchanged. An eternal figure who asks not for adoration, but for readiness. He is the ferryman of fate—the last companion, and the sentinel at the world's edge.

SYMBOL OF THE FINAL CROSSING

Across the ages and through the memory of myth, Charon has emerged as more than the ferryman of the dead. He is the very embodiment of transition. A spectral figure who exists between worlds, he represents fate's quiet hand guiding each departed soul toward what lies beyond. His presence reminds us that death is not an ending, but a crossing, one that demands preparation, respect, and the surrender of all earthly ties. In every retelling, from ancient verse to modern vision, Charon endures as a symbol of mortality's certainty and the soul's final rite of passage.

"No living soul may cross these waters' flow,
Until the silent coin is paid,
And the ferryman takes his due."
— Virgil, *Aeneid*

Cycle-Bearer of Death

Charon, the silent ferryman of the River Styx, stands not merely as a character in myth but as the living emblem of death's eternal rhythm. His passage across the dark waters mirrors the soul's departure from the world of light into the shadows beyond—a journey not abrupt, but sacred and inevitable. In Greek thought, death was not an end, but a passage; a shedding of form, a movement into mystery. Charon is the threshold incarnate, the one who ensures that this sacred transition proceeds undisturbed.

The coin offered to him was no trivial fee. It was a symbol of readiness—a final transaction that acknowledged life's completion and death's order. Without this fare, the soul could not proceed. Trapped in limbo, the unburied wandered, unfinished and unclaimed. Through this simple ritual, the Greeks affirmed that death, like life, was governed by divine law, and Charon was its enforcer. He did not pass judgment, but he did maintain the boundary—ensuring no soul crossed unbidden and no crossing went unpaid.

That Charon remains unchanged through centuries of myth speaks to the constancy of his role. Where other gods shifted, battled, or fell, Charon endured—his eyes dark, his voice absent, his duty unwavering. He is the quiet force behind the passage, a symbol not of punishment but of truth that all who live must one day cross, and all who cross must pay. His oar does not strike; it separates. His silence is not void, but certainty.

Across Time and Imagination

Charon, though born of ancient lore, has never faded into silence. His spectral silhouette still casts its shadow across literature, art, and popular imagination, proof that the archetype of the ferryman speaks to something endless in the human soul. In Roman mythology, Virgil's *Aeneid* reimagined him as a fierce and unrelenting guardian of the river, his words edged with celestial authority. In this portrayal, Charon becomes not only a servant of death, but its enforcer—terrifying, necessary, and absolute.

Dante's *Inferno* further transformed him into a wrathful demon, ferrying the damned across the River Acheron with curses on his lips. No longer a neutral figure of transition, Charon became a herald of torment, shaped by the Christian imagination into a gatekeeper of punishment. His myth was repurposed yet never erased, a testament to its enduring grip on the human psyche.

Even now, Charon's image endures in modern storytelling. From ancient verse to modern vision, from poets to painters, from stage to screen, the ferryman appears cloaked in mystery, guiding the departed across shadowed waters. Sometimes literal, sometimes metaphorical, his boat represents the crossing no mortal escapes. Through every retelling, Charon reminds us that the final journey is both sacred and shared—and that, no matter the age, the river still waits.

Final Companion Across Cultures

The figure of the ferryman is not confined to the banks of the Styx. Across many cultures and centuries, humanity has envisioned guardians who guide the dead from one world to the next—keepers of transition, bound not by name but by function. In ancient Egypt, the jackal-headed god Anubis led the departed to judgment, weighing their hearts against the feather of truth. Though Anubis was judge as well as guide, his role echoed that of Charon. A sacred custodian who ensured the soul did not stray from their destined path.

In the icy myths of the Norse, it was Hel who reigned over the dead—those who died not by blade, but by sickness or age. Her realm, shadowed and solemn, mirrored the Greek Underworld in its separation from the living. Though no ferryman stood at her gates, the theme remained. Death was a domain apart, and the passage to reach it required a custodian.

Even beyond folklore and myth, the archetype persists. The Grim Reaper, shrouded and skeletal, carries a scythe instead of an oar, but his role remains the same. He does not punish. He does not bless. He comes when called, and none may turn him away. In depth psychology, Carl Jung identified the ferryman as a symbol of transition—between life and death, childhood and maturity, ignorance and revelation. He is not just a figure of death, but of transformation.

Such enduring presence reveals a truth older than civilization. The need for one who waits at the edge. Whether through river or shadow, silence or song, there is always a guide who carries us forward when our final crossing must be made. In every culture, the soul seeks its passage—and the ferryman waits.

AT THE EDGE OF ETERNITY

Charon's duty was neither cruel nor compassionate, it was absolute. He judged no soul, nor guided any to paradise or punishment. He simply ferried them across the dark waters of the River Styx, ensuring the sacred threshold between the living and the dead remained inviolate. For those who arrived with offering, he was the keeper of passage. For those unprepared, he was a silent sentinel of denial, leaving them stranded in the misty shadows between breath and oblivion.

Yet Charon was no mere servant. He embodied the moment of transition itself. The crossing from one existence to another. His figure endured not because of dialogue or divinity, but because of what he represented. Inevitability, ritual, and the solemn truth that death comes for all. From Virgil's blazing-eyed boatman to Dante's infernal ferryman, from classical urns to digital screens, Charon's silhouette continues to haunt the threshold of our stories and our souls.

Still, every crossing must end upon a farther shore. Beyond that, a greater reckoning awaits. Upon the far side of the Styx stood three ancient judges, the final arbiters of a soul's fate. It was they who measured a life, weighed a soul, and chose a final path. In the next chapter, we pass into the solemn court of Rhadamanthus,

Aeacus, and Minos—where every soul stands beneath the gaze of the gods.

CHAPTER 5

JUDGES OF FATE

Rhadamanthus, Minos, and Aeacus

The Underworld was not chaos cloaked in darkness. It was a realm ruled by balance. Beneath the veils of shadow, where no crown or coin could sway destiny, every soul stood equal before judgment. Here, divine justice was not an abstract ideal but a destined force, upheld by the adjudicators of fate, Rhadamanthus, Aeacus, and Minos. These legendary judges, born of royal blood and hallowed legacy, weighed the lives of mortals with wisdom untouched by favor or fear. Each bore a sacred charge within Hades' kingdom, interpreting the unseen laws that governed the dead, and shaping each soul's fate with unerring resolve.

> *"There in the realm of Hades stand the judges of the dead,*
> *Wise Aeacus, stern Rhadamanthus, and mighty Minos,*
> *Weighing the fates of mortal souls with unerring justice."*
> — Pindar, *Olympian Odes*

Weighing the Soul

The Underworld was no wasteland of drifting spirits nor an emptiness of chaos. It was a realm bound by cosmic law, where the fate of every soul was measured with unwavering precision. Here, justice reigned, not by divine whim, but through the eternal vigilance of three immortal judges, Rhadamanthus, Minos, and Aeacus. They were no common figures, but once-mortal kings, chosen by the gods for their rare wisdom and incorruptible virtue. In death, they ascended to a higher calling, to pass judgment over the dead and assign each soul its rightful place in the afterlife.

Rhadamanthus, the most severe of the trio, was guardian of the righteous. It was he who examined lives lived with honor, offering passage to the Elysian Fields, a realm of golden light and endless harmony. His verdicts were swift and absolute—a voice of law that even the gods dared not challenge. Aeacus, esteemed for his fairness and clarity of mind, watched over the gates of the Underworld. It was said that he discerned the souls with ties to the gods, ensuring that even those touched by Olympus did not escape rightful scrutiny.

Above them stood Minos, not in height, but in finality. As chief among the judges, he rendered the last decision when the scales of justice wavered. He was the final word, the still center of the Underworld's sacred court. Together, these three formed a tribunal unlike any in myth or mortal law. A triad of balance, solemnity, and eternal duty. Through them, the kingdom of Hades upheld its order, ensuring that every soul, regardless of power or poverty in life, met its destiny with justice.

Final Reckoning

In the Underworld, judgment was not rushed nor swayed by influence, it was sacred, absolute, and unflinching. When a spirit arrived, stripped of flesh and pretense, it stood exposed before the three solemn judges. No lie could pass their gaze, for the very kingdom echoed with the truth of a soul's deeds. Every act, whether noble or vile, was drawn forth like breath from bone. The Underworld unveiled the whole of a life lived, leaving nothing hidden in shadow.

Those who had walked with honor—heroes, poets, and mortals who served the greater good—were granted passage to the Elysian Fields. There, in golden meadows untouched by sorrow, they would dwell in eternal light, free from the burdens of pain and mortality. For those whose lives had neither soared nor sunk, souls who committed no grave sin nor great virtue, they were consigned to the Asphodel Meadows, a quiet realm of soft gray and drifting memory. But for the wicked—the oath-breakers, the tyrants, the unjust—Tartarus awaited. That chasm of despair held punishments as fitting as they were merciless, carved from the shape of each soul's crime.

Yet the judges did not wield cruelty. Rhadamanthus, Minos, and Aeacus passed sentence not with wrath but with bound duty. They did not torment—they placed. Their hands did not punish—they ensured balance. In their rulings, the cosmos found order. Neither king nor deceiver could sway them. Before their thrones, all souls stood equal. And in that ceremonial stillness, justice was served, not for vengeance, but for harmony eternal.

Mortal Kings

It was no accident that the judges of the dead had once worn mortal crowns. In life, they ruled with wisdom and discipline, earning the esteem of gods and men alike. Their reigns upon the earth served as a foreshadowing of their immortal task, for just as they had governed mortal realms with justice, they were chosen to govern the dead with the same resolve. Their thrones were exchanged not for rest, but for the sanctified charge of preserving balance beyond the veil.

Rhadamanthus, the sternest of the three, was born of Zeus and Europa. As king of Crete, he became a living embodiment of law, unyielding in principle, yet revered for his fairness. Even in life, his name carried the weight of righteousness, and no transgression passed unseen beneath his watch. His brother Minos, also a son of

Zeus, ruled Crete and forged its laws with wisdom and force. Though remembered at times as severe, his brilliance in governance made him a fitting high judge among the dead. Aeacus, son of Zeus and the nymph Aegina, ruled over the island that bore his name. So great was his piety and discernment that even the gods sought his counsel, and in him, the spirit of hallowed justice found a mortal vessel.

Their elevation was no mere reward. It was a mantle of eternal duty. These kings, once bound by flesh and throne, now stood between worlds as arbiters of fate. They were not gods, nor fading phantoms, but something rarer. Immortal judges forged by the merit of their deeds. In their hands, the scales of the Underworld were held steady, and through them, the laws of death were preserved with the same stately dignity they had once brought to life.

The Last Word

The presence of Rhadamanthus, Minos, and Aeacus in the Underworld symbolized a truth that outlasted empires—justice endures. As eternal guardians, they stood at the threshold of providence, ensuring that every soul answered for its deeds, whether to receive reward or endure punishment. Their authority was unchallenged, their rulings final, shaped not by divine whim or mortal influence, but by an incorruptible sense of balance that even the gods respected.

Their role reflected the Greek conviction that character defined destiny. The belief that one's actions in life determined one's judgement in death reinforced the sacred value placed on virtue— on integrity, honor, and piety. The judges reminded mortals that justice was not bound to the living. It followed the soul beyond the grave, waiting silently in the dark, where fairness was no longer a matter of opinion but of truth revealed.

Though the judges seldom stood at the center of myth, their presence was a constant force—quiet, impartial, and immovable. They were the hidden pillars of order within a realm that could easily collapse into chaos. Where other gods might rule with force or desire, the final arbiters ruled through judgment, meting out justice without favor or fear. In this, they became the true keepers of the Underworld, not through crowns or thrones, but through unyielding law.

Their names may not resound with the same thunder as Hades or Persephone, but their role was no less sacred. They were the arbiters of destiny, unseen yet ever-present, determining the eternal path of every soul that crossed the River Styx. In the shadowed halls of the dead, their verdicts echoed without end, preserving the fragile balance between judgment and mercy, chaos and order, life and the quiet beyond.

Yet judgment itself was but the threshold—for beyond their verdicts lay the realms where fate was fulfilled.

SCALES OF THE FINAL TRIBUNAL

The kingdom of Hades was not a realm of chaos—where the destiny of every soul was decided with solemn precision. Upon death, each spirit stood before the three eternal judges—Minos, Rhadamanthus, and Aeacus—who weighed the truth of their lives. No lie could veil a soul's deeds, and no favor could sway fate. The righteous found endless joy in Elysium. The ordinary wandered the ashen fields of Asphodel. The wicked fell into Tartarus, where the

Furies meted out divine punishment. Justice in the world of Hades was final and incorruptible, a mirror of mortal virtue and vice.

> *"There Minos, golden scepter in hand,*
> *Judges the dead, seated, shaking the urn,*
> *Weighing their lives, deciding their fates."*
> — Homer, *Odyssey*

Decree of the Silent Kings

Upon crossing into the Underworld, every soul met a moment of unflinching reckoning. No mortal—king or beggar, hero or traitor—could escape the gaze of judgment. The three great judges stood before them, their eyes seeing not flesh or fame, but the truth that clung to every life lived.

Some accounts speak of a great scale upon which a soul's deeds were weighed, not as in the Egyptian rite of the feather, but through the discerning eyes of Rhadamanthus, Minos, and Aeacus. Virtue and vice, justice and cruelty—each was considered part of the soul's legacy. With solemn authority, the judges rendered their verdict.

The righteous, whose lives bore courage, honor, and reverence for the gods, were granted passage to Elysium, a realm of eternal peace. The ordinary, neither evil nor exalted, were sent to the Asphodel Meadows to drift in quiet reflection. But for the corrupt—the oathbreakers, tyrants, and blasphemers, Tartarus awaited, a prison of eternal consequence, where punishment matched the weight of their misdeeds.

Handmaidens of Vengeance

Though the judges cast the verdict, it was the Furies who ensured it was obeyed. Born from the blood of Uranus and forged in the oldest fires of wrath, these fearsome spirits haunted the depths of the Underworld, enforcing celestial justice with unrelenting fury. Where judgment ended, their work began. No soul condemned to Tartarus could escape the punishment they delivered. Not even the gods dared to stand in their way.

Wreathed in serpents, cloaked in shadow, and driven by an ancient sense of purpose, the Furies fell upon the wicked with merciless precision. Oath-breakers, kin-slayers, blasphemers— none were spared. Their torments were tailored to the crime. The greedy were left forever famished before unreachable banquets; the traitorous, pursued by the voices of the dead they had betrayed. Their punishments were not cruel, but balance. Each lash of suffering echoed the weight of broken laws and shattered bonds.

Yet the reach of the Furies did not end in the domain of the dead. When sacred crimes stained the world above, they rose from the depths to hunt the living, driving the guilty to madness, exile, or self-destruction, until the soul was delivered to its final sentence. They were not demons, but ordained arbiters of vengeance— sacred, inexorable, and terrifying. Even Hades himself, ruler of the dead, dared not restrain them. For the Furies answered only to the cosmos, guardians of a truth older than Olympus, that justice must not only be spoken, but fulfilled.

Destinies Beyond Death

With judgment rendered and fate decreed, each soul began its final journey across the Underworld's shadowed terrain. Those deemed worthy of godly reward were led to Elysium, a land of golden fields bathed in everlasting sunlight, where the air shimmered with song and the blessed lived in peace beyond sorrow. Here dwelled the heroes, the just, and the pious—those who had honored the gods and upheld virtue in life. In this paradise of music, feasting, and unbroken joy, the soul knew no regret. Some, filled with longing for even greater glory, chose rebirth, hoping to earn their place in Elysium again and again until they transcended the mortal cycle forever.

Yet most souls were neither saint nor sinner. For these, the journey ended in the Asphodel Meadows—a vast, gray expanse where the ordinary dead lingered in gentle obscurity. It was not a place of torment, but neither did it offer delight. Beneath a sky without color, these souls wandered in reflection, their memories slowly fading, their voices reduced to whispers. They were the countless unnamed, the farmers and soldiers, the mothers and merchants, lives lived without renown or disgrace, now drifting in the quiet stillness of eternity.

But for the most vile, those who had defied sacred oaths, betrayed kin, or mocked the gods, their path plunged into Tartarus. This abyss was no common prison, but a a world of ceaseless torment, where punishment mirrored the depth of one's transgressions. Sisyphus, who dared to outwit death, strained endlessly beneath a boulder that betrayed him with every step. Tantalus, cursed with hunger and thirst he could never quench, stood beneath fruit he could not reach. Ixion, the traitor who sought to seduce Hera, spun eternally upon a flaming wheel, his crime seared into the void itself.

There was no escape from Tartarus. No plea, no offering, no divine mercy could undo the sentence of a soul cast into its depths.

In this place, justice did not forget. It endured. Unlike the mortal world, where power might conceal guilt, the Underworld offered no such shelter. Here, the reckoning was final, and every punishment eternal, a solemn reminder that even in death, the laws of the cosmos held sway.

Final Measure

The judgment of the dead marked the final threshold—a solemn reckoning governed by balance, justice, and divine law. The hands of the three justices, Rhadamanthus, Minos, and Aeacus, did not waver. Their verdicts placed the departed where it belonged, rewarding virtue with peace and condemning sin with suffering. The Furies, relentless agents of justice, carried out these sentences with sacred precision, ensuring that none who defied the cosmic order escaped its wrath.

Yet within this unyielding system lay a mirror of mortal existence, a truth both ancient and eternal. Every choice echoes beyond the grave. The Underworld, for all its shadows, reflected the lives once lived. Whether destined for paradise, lost to limbo, or cast into torment, each soul found its rightful place, its fate bound not by chance, but by the weight of its deeds and the laws it dared to uphold—or break.

DIVINE JUSTICE

Across myth and history, the judgment of souls stood as both a moral compass and a spiritual mirror. In the Greek tradition, it was not merely the dead who were judged, but the living who were warned. Through the vigilance of Rhadamanthus, Minos, and Aeacus, the Underworld offered a vision of justice that outlived the grave. This belief, that mortal deeds outlast the grave, shaped civilizations that followed, inspiring the tribunals of Plato, the visions of Dante, and the doctrines of faiths yet to come. In every age, the soul is measured by an order it cannot escape.

> *"But when the spirits of the dead arrive before them,*
> *Rhadamanthus holds their judgment,*
> *And punishes the guilty, teaching them*
> *the penalty for their misdeeds."*
> — Plato, *Gorgias*

Sacred Balance

In the world of Greek mythology, justice was no idle abstraction. It was a sacred force woven into the fabric of existence, watched over by divine eyes and weighed by eternal laws. Mortals did not act unseen—every deed left an imprint, every choice echoed in the afterlife. The three judges of the Underworld ensured that those echoes were heard. In their hands, every crime was seen, every virtue remembered. Through them, the will of the gods took form, measuring each spirit not by status or strength, but by the truth of their actions.

Unlike the Olympians, whose passions often blurred the lines of justice, the Underworld's judgment remained impersonal and pure. It sought not vengeance, but equilibrium. The virtuous were welcomed into Elysium, their reward a peace earned by righteousness. The evil, those who defied oaths or spilled innocent blood, were condemned not by malice but by necessity, to restore the balance they had broken. In this realm beneath the earth, justice moved with precision, unswayed by plea or power.

This belief in hallowed accountability shaped Greek thought far beyond the grave. It breathed through their laws, infused their tragedies, and echoed in the teachings of their philosophers. To live with honor was not merely to win praise in life, but to secure one's place in eternity. The judgment of the dead reminded all who lived that the soul's true weight would be known at the end—that beyond the applause of kings or the envy of rivals, only justice endured.

The Soul Revealed

Ancient voices offered differing visions of the Underworld and the judgments that awaited the dead, each reflecting the evolving moral and spiritual landscape of Greece. Homer, in *The Odyssey*, painted the afterlife as a dim and desolate realm—a mist-bound domain where all souls, noble and base alike, drifted as shades. Yet even within this somber vision, Minos appears seated in judgment, settling disputes among the dead. His presence suggests that justice endured beyond the grave, even if the rewards and punishments were not yet fully defined.

Virgil, writing centuries later, gave the Underworld solemn structure and sacred purpose. Here, judgment was no distant concept but a divine tribunal. Rhadamanthus loomed as an unrelenting interrogator, laying bare the sins of the soul before assigning its eternal fate—paradise for the virtuous, torment for the wicked. In Virgil's world, the afterlife reflected a moral cosmos, where actions in life shaped one's eternity, and judgment became the fulcrum upon which the soul's destiny turned.

In the philosophical realm of Plato, judgment transcended myth and became metaphor. In *Gorgias*, he described the soul's unveiling—the stripping away of mortal illusion and the confrontation with eternal truth. The judges, once mortal kings, now rendered verdicts with godly insight, untouched by persuasion or deceit. Plato's vision was not just of vengeance or reward, but of moral clarity, a reckoning that revealed the soul's true weight. Through his lens, the Underworld was not simply a world of the dead, but a crucible of ethical consequence.

These ancient interpretations form a chorus of belief, a progression from shadowy existence to divine order, from wandering spirits to souls held accountable. Across ages and empires, that vision of justice took new form, yet one truth endured. The soul could never escape the measure of its own deeds.

Across Realms and Faiths

Though the Greek vision of celestial judgment was singular in its formality and symbolism, the concept of moral reckoning after death echoed across civilizations. From the deserts of Egypt to the icy reaches of the North, ancient cultures wrestled with the same eternal question. What becomes of the soul once life has passed?

In Egyptian mythology, the afterlife was governed by the sacred rite known as the Weighing of the Heart. Before the throne of Osiris, the lord of the dead, a soul's heart was placed upon the scale and balanced against a feather the symbol of Ma'at, the cosmic order. If the heart proved heavy with wrongdoing, it was cast to Ammit, the devourer, and the soul ceased to be. But if it was found pure, the soul passed into the Field of Reeds, a paradise of eternal peace. Unlike the Greek tribunal of kings, the Egyptian judgment was swift, solitary, and final, an act of divine measurement, not deliberation.

In the sagas of Norse mythology, judgment was veiled, yet ever-present. The slain who met death with valor were chosen by Odin, carried by Valkyries to Valhalla, where they would feast until the twilight of the gods. Those who died without glory descended into Helheim, a somber realm under the gaze of Hel, daughter of Loki. Though not bound by trials or judges, Norse belief still held the notion that honor in life shaped one's fate in death, a quieter form of judgment, carried on the breath of battle and legacy.

In Christian thought, divine judgment became deeply personal. Each soul, upon death, stood before the Creator, their faith and deeds laid bare. Paradise and damnation awaited, mirroring the Greek Elysium and Tartarus, yet infused with themes of grace, mercy, and eternal redemption. The Last Judgment, where all souls would be called and judged together, reflected a vision of cosmic justice forged from ancient roots, refined by centuries of reflection and theology.

Across mythologies, the soul is never cast adrift. Whether weighed, summoned, or silently chosen, its passage is marked by consequence. In every tradition, the message endures that the life one leads does not vanish into silence. It echoes into eternity.

Voices of the Afterlife

The myths of the Greek Underworld did not fade into the dust of antiquity. They became the scaffolding upon which later civilizations built their visions of divine judgment. The moral architecture forged by the great judges of the dead, where every soul was weighed, and fate was earned, echoed far beyond Greece, shaping theology, literature, and law across centuries.

Christianity, though rooted in its own sacred texts, absorbed and reimagined many of these ancient ideas. The division between heaven and hell, the concept of a final reckoning, and the belief that each soul's destiny is shaped by its earthly deeds all mirror the judgments of Elysium, Asphodel, and Tartarus. Dante's *Inferno*, guided by Virgil himself, stands as a monumental testament to this inheritance. With its layered punishments and moral logic, it transforms myth into theology, casting Greek structure into a Christian frame.

These beliefs did not remain bound to religion alone. In medieval and Renaissance thought, the soul's accountability found voice in legal systems and philosophical treatises. The eternal nature of justice that no action is without consequence, and no life escapes final accounting, permeated ethics, literature, and the governance of kingdoms. Even in today's secular reflections, echoes of these myths remain. The conviction that truth will be known, that justice outlives death, and that morality is written not just in law, but in eternity.

Through their stories, the Greeks gave us more than a map of the afterlife. They gave us a mirror for the soul. The judges of the dead live on not only in the myths we retell, but in the values we uphold, the questions we still ask, and the conscience that guides us through the shadowed corridors of mortality itself.

VERDICT BEYOND LIFE

The three judges of the dead—Rhadamanthus, Minos, and Aeacus—stood as arbiters of fate, ensuring that every soul received the destiny it had earned. Their presence in the Underworld embodied the Greek ideal of divine justice, where the deeds of mortals—whether noble or wicked— defined the contours of their eternity. Through their unwavering judgment, balance was preserved. The righteous found peace in Elysium, the ordinary drifted through the gray expanse of the Asphodel Meadows, and the condemned were cast into the torments of Tartarus.

Yet judgment was not the journey's end. For those consigned to Tartarus, justice did not merely sever them from the world of the living. It transformed their guilt into suffering, their transgressions into eternal sentence. What awaited below was not a mere punishment, but reflection made into agony. In the next chapter, we descend into that abyss, where the proud and the defiant meet their fates, and the legends of Sisyphus, Tantalus, and others stand as immortal testaments to the cost of defiance and the reach of divine wrath.

CHAPTER 6

TORMENTS OF TARTARUS

![Sinners of the Underworld illustration]

Sinners of the Underworld

In the deepest reaches of the Underworld lay Tartarus—not disorder, but design made perpetual. Here, divine justice carved eternity into suffering. The souls confined to this abyss were no common wrongdoers, but beings whose defiance had shattered sacred law. Each torment mirrored its crime; each agony a reflection of disobedience repaid. Pride, betrayal, and blasphemy did not go unmarked. In this depth, sin became sentence, and pain endured as monument to the divine.

> *"There in the Underworld, the wicked*
> *endure endless torment,'*
> *Bound by chains, lamenting their fate,*
> *As justice decrees the penalty for their crimes."*
> — Hesiod, *Theogony*

Burden of Defiance

Sisyphus, once king among mortals, mocked the order of the cosmos with cunning born of hubris. He betrayed sacred guest-right, deceived the gods, and in ultimate defiance bound Thanatos himself, halting death and unraveling the mortal cycle. For such opposition of divine law, his sentence was carved into eternity.

Condemned to a torment of perfect futility, Sisyphus labors beneath the weight of a massive stone, straining up the face of an endless slope. Yet each time the summit nears, the boulder slips from his grasp and crashes below. His agony is not pain, but purpose denied. His toil is a monument to pride undone, an echo that endures where mortal will met hallowed order and broke.

Hunger Beyond Redemption

Tantalus had once walked among the gods, a mortal king honored at their celestial table. But reverence gave way to arrogance, and in pride he stained the venerated order. In a perverse test of the gods' omniscience, he slew his own son and served the flesh at a divine feast. The immortals, discerning and horrified, restored the boy to life and cast Tantalus into the abyss as warning eternal.

In Tartarus, he stood in a pool of cool water, yet each time he stooped to drink, it withdrew. Above him hung branches heavy with golden fruit, yet they rose at every reach. Surrounded by plenty, he starved; enveloped in promise, he thirsted. His punishment was the mirror of his sin. Abundance turned to torment, hunger made holy in its justice.

Bound to the Flame

Ixion, a mortal king of proud descent, was welcomed to Olympus as guest of Zeus. Granted a seat among the immortals, a gift few had known, he answered favor with desire. His eyes turned to Hera, queen of the gods. Zeus, reading the treachery of his heart, forged a phantom in Hera's likeness and set the snare. Ixion's fall was swift, his shame complete.

For lust against divinity and betrayal of sacred hospitality, Ixion was hurled into Tartarus. There he was bound to a blazing wheel that spun through the void, fire licking his flesh yet never consuming it. Each revolution was confession. Each flame, remembrance. His fate became motion without mercy, a warning written in light and pain that no mortal may covet the divine.

Ashes of a Pretender

Salmoneus, a king consumed by vanity, did not merely defy the gods. He dared to impersonate them. Proclaiming himself Zeus, he rode through his city in a bronze chariot, its wheels clattering like false thunder as he hurled torches to mimic lightning. But imitation of the gods demands its price.

From his throne above, Zeus cast a single, true bolt. It tore the heavens and struck Salmoneus down, his false thunder silenced in fire. Yet death was no release. In Tartarus, illusions of power forever receded before him. Each time he reached for godhood, he fell anew. His torment echoed through the abyss, a cycle of arrogance and ruin, proof that no mortal may wear the storm's crown. Thus pride took many forms, but each found the same end, submission before divine order.

Fate of the Fifty Sisters

The Danaids, fifty daughters of Danaus, were bound by blood and betrayal. Ordered to wed the fifty sons of Aegyptus, they obeyed their father's dreadful command and slew their husbands on their wedding night—all but Hypermnestra, who chose mercy over murder.

For this collective crime, the sisters were cast into Tartarus. Each was given a vessel to fill with water, but the jars were pierced, leaking endlessly. Century after century, they labored. Every drop undone by its own escape. Their punishment was obedience turned to futility, loyalty made void. In the hush of their toil, their whispers still warn. Blood may command, but justice alone absolves.

The Eternal Lessons of Tartarus

The punishments of Tartarus were verdicts sculpted from the sin itself. Sisyphus, deceiver, was chained to fruitless labor. Tantalus, betrayer of sacred trust, starved beneath abundance. Ixion, whose desire defied Olympus, burned upon the wheel. Salmoneus, mocker of Zeus, relived false glory and divine scorn. The Danaids, killers bound by duty, toiled in futility without end.

Each fate was not cruelty, but consequence, law taking shape in suffering. Tartarus remembered every oath, every trespass. Here, justice was not written but lived, sin made form, punishment made eternal. The abyss stood as the dark heart of balance, where divine order endured, unbending and complete.

DECREES OF THE IMMORTALS

In the mythic order of ancient Greece, punishment was not vengeance, but balance. Mortal transgressions rippled beyond death, drawing the attention of gods who guarded the boundaries of the cosmos. When those lines were crossed, the sentence was swift and sacred. Divine punishment reinforced the laws that separated gods from men, reminding mortals of their place in the eternal design. Though often severe, damnation was never without purpose. They taught the price of hubris, the sanctity of oaths, and the weight of justice—and in rare cases, they whispered of redemption through suffering.

"For those who have committed unrighteous deeds,
Retribution follows them in the halls of Hades,
And justice is meted out, unyielding and severe."
— Plato, *Phaedo*

Price of Defying Olympus

The Olympians were not only rulers of the heavens, but stewards of sacred law, enforcers of the cosmic order that governed both mortal and immortal. When a mortal transgressed that order through hubris, defiance, or sacrilege, retribution was swift and merciless. These actions were not random displays of wrath but hallowed declarations, lessons carved into myth, reminders of humanity's place beneath the heavens.

Among the gravest offenses was hubris, the mortal sin of challenging the gods. Queen Niobe, who dared compare herself to Leto, watched her children struck down by Apollo and Artemis, her pride drowned in grief until she was turned to stone, frozen in weeping for eternity. Prometheus, the titan who defied Zeus to gift fire to mankind, was chained to a desolate rock, his immortal flesh torn and devoured each day by a sacred eagle. Their punishments were not merely suffering. They were poetic reflections of crime, where arrogance begot agony, and rebellion birthed endless loss.

Not all offenses, however, were direct affronts to the gods. Some violated sacred bonds—of kinship, oath, or hospitality. Tantalus, who served his own son as a meal to the gods of Olympus, was cast into Tartarus, where fruit and water forever eluded his reach. These stories upheld a divine truth that some acts, no matter how hidden in life, would find judgment in death, and the gods would ensure that no sacred law remained unavenged.

Lessons in Divine Justice

Though the torments of Tartarus were cruel and unrelenting, they served a purpose beyond mere vengeance. Each myth stood as a sanctified warning, carved into eternity to remind mortals of the boundaries they must not cross. These punishments reflected a moral order where no transgression escaped notice, and where the gods' justice endured beyond death.

Sisyphus's endless labor became a parable for the futility of deception. His opposition of death earned him not freedom, but a sentence that mirrored his cunning—eternal exertion without reward. Ixion's fate, spinning upon a flaming wheel, embodied the consequences of betrayal and unchecked ambition. Each punishment was symbolic, not just of guilt, but of the lesson it imposed.

Greek mythology did more than entertain. It preserved the sacred pillars of culture. Hospitality, loyalty, and reverence for the gods were ordained virtues. The Danaids, condemned to fill leaking jars, paid not just for murder, but for the betrayal of sacred bonds. Their punishment taught that even obedience to mortal commands could not excuse violation of divine law.

In the end, punishment was never random. It upheld balance. The Underworld itself—divided into paradise, limbo, and torment—reflected a cosmos ordered by justice, where every soul received the fate its life had earned.

Redemption Beyond the Abyss

Though Tartarus echoed with endless cries, not every soul condemned to its depths was lost forever. In certain myths, redemption shimmered like a distant flame—faint, flickering, yet never fully extinguished. These rare tales spoke of atonement forged through suffering, of purification through pain, and of a soul's ascent from darkness into light.

The Orphic Mysteries, cloaked in sacred secrecy, whispered of such paths. They taught that the soul, though bound by its deeds, could be cleansed across lifetimes. Rebirth offered the weary spirit a chance to rise anew, each cycle of life a crucible through which wisdom and virtue might be reclaimed. In these traditions, Elysium was not merely a reward, but destination—reached through perseverance and moral awakening.

Even in the rigid framework of celestial justice, mercy stirred. Heracles, hero of trials and bearer of burdens, descended into the Underworld and lifted Theseus from the shadows, winning pardon from the very gods who had condemned him. Plato, in his visions of the soul's journey, saw punishment not only as retribution but as instruction, a sorrow that could lead to insight. In this vision, the Underworld was not the end of hope, but the beginning of understanding.

Last Light in the Deepest Dark

Punishment in Greek mythology was never wielded solely as a weapon of fear. It was moral instruction, revealing the eternal dance between justice and consequence. The torments of Tartarus were carved not from cruelty, but from cosmic order. Each fate served as a mirror, reflecting the shadows of human nature. Pride untempered, loyalty betrayed, and oaths defiled. These tales were not warnings alone, but truths reminding mortals that every action rippled beyond death.

Yet even in the blackest corners of the Underworld, the myths whispered of mercy. Rare though it was, redemption stood as a counterweight to punishment, proof that the divine could be moved by understanding, not only law. The presence of such grace did not diminish justice. It completed it, showing that the gods were not bound by wrath alone, but by a deeper harmony.

In the mythic design of existence, punishment was not an end. It was a passage. No sin was forgotten, but neither was the soul forsaken. The legends of Tartarus remind us that the scales of fate held room not only for judgment, but for the possibility that wisdom could rise from suffering, and light could break even the most unyielding dark.

WHERE SHADOWS STILL WHISPER

Tartarus—eternal, unyielding, veiled in shadow—has endured beyond the myths of ancient Greece. It shaped visions of hell, colored portrayals of the afterlife, and became a symbol of cosmic retribution. From classical verse to modern fantasy, from allegory to horror, it survives as a mythic echo, a prison for those who defy divine law, and a mirror of human guilt, fear, and consequence. Tartarus is not merely a place—it is a legacy of suffering, a reminder that in every age, some sins still scream from the depths.

> *"Far below the house of Hades,*
> *as far beneath as heaven is above the earth,*
> *Lies Tartarus, wrapped in mist and gloom,*
> *A prison for those who have defied the will of the gods."*
> — Homer, *Iliad*

Tartarus Reborn

The image of Tartarus as a dominion of endless torment has echoed through centuries of storytelling, shaping visions of punishment, morality, and the afterlife in literature, film, and popular culture. From Virgil to Dante, poets and prophets alike reshaped Tartarus within their own spiritual frameworks. Virgil's *Aeneid* depicted Tartarus as a vast and dreadful prison for the evil, while Dante's *Inferno* transformed it into layered rings of torment, echoing the poetic justice of ancient Greek punishment.

In modern fiction, Tartarus has found new life in fantasy and horror. In *Percy Jackson & the Olympians*, Rick Riordan revives Tartarus not only as a place, but as a conscious, malevolent entity, ensuring the abyss retains its ancient menace. J.R.R. Tolkien's Void in *The Silmarillion*, where Melkor is cast for his crimes, mirrors the cosmic exile of the Titans, reinforcing Tartarus's influence beyond Greek borders.

Across ages—through film, art, and story—Tartarus endures. From *Clash of the Titans* to *God of War*, and in the mythological threads of Wonder Woman's DC universe, the vast abyss remains a vessel of fear and consequence. Whether imagined as a prison, a battlefield, or a sentient force, Tartarus still whispers from the edge of imagination, reminding all that certain sins still awaken eternal echoes.

Underworlds of Humankind

The vision of Tartarus—eternal, absolute, and unyielding—was a uniquely Greek conception. Yet the belief in a realm where the vile are judged and punished after death echoes across the mythologies of the world. From the mists of Niflhel to the blazing chambers of Naraka, ancient cultures gave form to their fears, their justice, and their hope through stories of the afterlife's darkest domains.

In Christian theology, Tartarus finds its closest reflection in Hell. Shaped by doctrine and deepened by Dante and Milton, Hell is imagined as a place of tiered torments, where each sin reaps its own punishment. Like Tartarus, it is a land of retribution, where cosmic order is restored through suffering. The idea that punishment must mirror crime, so central to Greek thought, carries into this vision of endless damnation.

In the Norse tradition, those who die dishonorably are denied entry to Valhalla and instead, descend into Niflhel. Ruled by the cold and distant goddess Hel, this shadowed land serves not as fire but as frost, a place of bleak stillness and shame. Here, as in Tartarus, punishment is not merely a sentence, but a severing of one's heroic potential and divine favor.

In Hindu and Buddhist cosmology, Naraka offers a realm of torment shaped by karmic law. Yet unlike Tartarus, its punishments are not forever. Souls suffer until their debts are paid and then, they may be reborn. This vision introduces the possibility of redemption through endurance, a path denied to most in Greek myth, where divine judgment, once passed, is rarely revoked.

Through all these traditions, a shared truth emerges that the cosmos demands balance, and that justice stretches beyond the grave. Whether carved in fire, frozen in ice, or weighed by karma, the punishment of the soul speaks to the moral fabric of the universe. And though Tartarus stands apart in its finality, it joins a chorus of eternal realms that whisper one immutable law. Every deed echoes beyond death.

Myths of the Abyss

Tartarus, once imagined as a distant abyss beneath the earth, has endured not only as a mythic prison but as a potent symbol of the human condition. In modern thought, it no longer resides solely beneath the world but within it, reflected in the silent agonies of the soul. For many, Tartarus is not a place, but a state of being, a world of regret, guilt, and relentless inner trial.

Psychologically, Tartarus mirrors the cycles of trauma and self-condemnation. Just as Sisyphus strains endlessly beneath the weight of his burden, those haunted by shame or sorrow push against invisible stones of their own making. The punishments of myth, crafted to match the sin, now echo as metaphors for the way the mind replays its errors, crafting prisons from memory and remorse.

Philosophers such as Camus have drawn from these ancient patterns to reflect on life's meaning amid suffering. In *The Myth of Sisyphus*, he envisions defiance not as escape but as endurance, an existential triumph in continuing the struggle. Through this lens, Tartarus becomes more than a place of despair; it becomes the forge of resilience, where the spirit endures not despite absurdity, but because of it.

Literature and cinema have also seized upon Tartarus as a metaphor for psychological and societal confinement. In Orwell's *1984*, never-ending surveillance and mental submission evoke the same unending torment seen in the myths. In *The Shawshank Redemption*, the prison becomes a symbolic Tartarus, where time itself punishes, and hope alone offers deliverance from despair.

This transformation of Tartarus, from chasm to concept, has only deepened its power. Its shadows now stretch across the human psyche, symbolizing the burdens we carry, the cycles we repeat, and the endurance we summon to rise. In this way, the oldest depths of Greek mythology still speak with relevance, reminding us that some Underworlds are walked not in death, but in life.

Weight of the Unforgotten

Tartarus has long outlived its mythic origins, becoming a symbol that speaks to more than punishment alone. From ancient verse to modern minds, it embodies the weight of justice, the sting of regret, and the haunting echo of choice. Whether portrayed as a realm beneath the earth or a darkness within the soul, Tartarus endures. It reminds us that some lessons are not simply learned, but lived—again and again, in myth and memory.

SILENCE AFTER JUDGEMENT

Tartarus stood as the final warning , a monument to divine reckoning. Here, punishment was not born of blind wrath, but of reflection—the echo of sin made manifest. Sisyphus strained beneath the weight of deceit. Tantalus starved amid abundance he had profaned. Ixion burned upon his wheel for betraying sacred trust. Each torment was carved with merciless precision, not from cruelty, but from balance, the unflinching symmetry between offense and fate.

Yet Tartarus was but one shadowed province in the vast dominion of Hades. It was the end of judgment, but not the fullness of the Underworld's truth. Beyond its flaming depths stretched meadows of silence, rivers of memory, and gates guarded by beasts and spirits. The order of the dead did not rest on punishment alone—it was sustained by those who upheld its law.

As we rise from the abyss, our path turns toward the keepers of that order—the guardians, spirits, and monstrous sentinels who stand at the boundaries of worlds. In their presence, the Underworld revealed its full form, not merely a kingdom of endings, but a realm of structure, balance, and divine design.

CHAPTER 7

SPIRITS, CREATURES, AND GUARDIANS

![Furies illustration]

Furies – Judgement Without Mercy

The Furies—called the Erinyes by the ancients—were not merely spirits of vengeance, but sacred instruments of hallowed law. Born from the blood of Uranus spilled upon the earth, they rose as keepers of the moral order, their wrath reserved for crimes that shattered the holy bonds of kinship, oath, and blood. Cloaked in shadow and crowned with serpents, they hunted the guilty without rest, a storm that crossed both land and soul. No plea could soften them, no sanctuary conceal the condemned. They answered not to mercy, but to truth. And in the dark courts of the Underworld, they stood as a warning. No injustice, no matter how deeply buried, would go unanswered.

> *"With unwearied speed they pursue the transgressor,*
> *Swift as stormy winds across the earth,*
> *Bringing vengeance upon those who defy the eternal laws."*
> — Aeschylus, *Eumenides*

Enforcers of Justice

Unlike the shades who dwelled in silence below, the Furies crossed the veil with ease. They hunted the living as fiercely as the dead, pursuing the oath-breaker, the traitor, the slayer of kin. No temple barred them, no plea recalled them. Where justice faltered, they became its hand—swift, incorruptible, and unrelenting.

The Furies were the breath of celestial order made wrath, a reminder that balance, once broken, demanded repair. Their wings beat like storm winds, their cries echoed through conscience itself. Wherever truth was buried, they unearthed it. Wherever guilt denied itself, they answered.

Punishment of the Forsworn

In the ancient world, an oath was a sacred vessel, sealed by the gods, binding mortal to immortal. To break one was to wound the fabric of the cosmos itself. And when such vows were broken, the Furies answered.

They descended upon the perjured with merciless precision, driving the guilty to madness or condemning them to fates shaped by their deceit. Their justice rang through the legend of Orestes, the son who avenged his father's murder by slaying his mother, Clytemnestra. Though his act obeyed Apollo's command, the Spirits of Retribution would not forgive the blood of the parent spilled by the child. They pursued him across earth and shadow until Athena herself convened judgment in Athens. There, beneath the eyes of gods and mortals, the Furies revealed the purity of their law. Even divine sanction could not silence the cry of violated blood.

The Avengers of Blood spared no king, no lineage. Their pursuit was principle made flesh, a living decree that none, not even the favored of Olympus, could rise above justice.

Unyielding Three

Though clothed in terror, the Furies were not cruel. They punished to restore, not to destroy. Known to the Greeks as the Erinyes, or Angry Ones, they embodied the sacred rage of the cosmos, a force summoned whenever balance was broken.

In the oldest myths, the Servants of Justice were countless, a storm of wings sweeping the guilty from the earth. Later, they took three enduring forms. There was Alecto, the Unceasing Anger; Megaera, the Jealous Rage; and Tisiphone, the Avenger of Murder.

Together they moved as one—terrible, necessary, and feared even by Zeus himself.

Their wrath could be transfigured. When Athena intervened in Orestes' trial, she tempered vengeance with mercy, renaming them Eumenides, or Kindly Ones. In that act, justice evolved. The Furies, once pure retribution, became guardians of reconciliation. Their fury remained, but its purpose was renewed.

Watchers of the Unatoned

The Furies stood as never-ending symbols of the bond between deed and consequence. They were not phantoms of vengeance, but living law, manifestations of a universe where no betrayal escaped remembrance. Their pursuit was not personal. It was principle itself.

To the guilty, they were nightmares woven from conscience and godly wrath—inescapable, unrelenting. To the wronged, they were sacred avengers, proof that fate was not blind, and chaos not sovereign.

As long as oaths were broken and sacred bonds betrayed, the Furies would endure—watching, waiting, ensuring that justice, though delayed, would never die.

GHOSTS OF THE UNDERWORLD

Not all spirits in Greek mythology found peace beyond the veil. Many lingered as shadows, pale echoes of life, stripped of voice and form, wandering the dim corridors of Hades. These shades, neither fully dead nor wholly gone, haunted the kingdom below with memories unfulfilled. Some were silent witnesses to eternity, others summoned by rites or prophecy, and a few remained tethered to the living world, bound by unfinished destiny. They were not forgotten, for in their silence lay the thinnest thread between life and death, a reminder that even in death, the soul remembers.

"There in the land of shadows stand the souls of the dead,
Fluttering like phantoms, voiceless and pale,
Wandering in the gloom, longing for the warmth of life."
— Homer, *Odyssey*

Souls and Shades

In Greek belief, the soul, or psyche, was the breath of life, departing the body at death and descending into the shadows of the Underworld. Yet not all spirits arrived whole. Many faded into shades, hollow imprints of who they had been, drifting through the gloom like shadowed smoke. Stripped of voice, passion, and memory, these wraiths wandered nameless through Hades' realm, echoes of lives they no longer held.

Unlike heroes who retained self and stature beyond death, most mortals dissolved into obscurity. Even Achilles, once the mightiest of warriors, was said to grieve his providence as a shade, lamenting that he would rather serve among the living than reign among the dead. Bound by laws older than Olympus, their serendipity was etched by mortal deed and divine decree.

And yet, some remnants stirred with purpose. Those who died unburied, betrayed, or violently wronged were not so easily silenced. Haunting the threshold between life and death, they cried for justice, remembrance, or release. With offerings, some were granted fleeting presence, summoned through sacred rites. In their unrest, the veil thinned, reminding the living that peace, like death, must be earned. Yet some found voice again—drawn upward by blood and invocation.

Voices Drawn by Blood

Though the Underworld was sealed to the living, there existed rites by which the boundary of souls could be pierced. Necromancy, known to the Greeks as nekyia, was a sacred and perilous act, calling forth the spirits of the departed through ritual, invocation, and blood. To summon the dead was not merely to speak with ghosts, but to trespass against the divine order, risking the wrath of specters and gods alike.

The most haunting account of such a rite appears in Homer's *Odyssey*, where Odysseus, seeking the counsel of Tiresias, travels to the edge of the world. There, beneath the bleak sky, he carves a trench in the earth and pours the blood of sacrifice. Drawn by the scent of life, the shades rise in droves, silent and starved. Only after drinking the blood do they speak, revealing truths veiled in shadow, foretelling what lies ahead.

But such rites were not performed lightly. A misstep in the ritual could unleash chaos—souls unbound, voices unending. Even outside myth, the Greeks honored the dead through offerings of honey, wine, and milk, whispered prayers at tombs, and festivals like the Anthesteria. The dead were not gone. They watched from beyond, waiting, remembered in silence and shadow.

Afterlife Without Passage

Ghosts held a solemn and enduring place in the beliefs of ancient Greece, embodying both a reverence for the past and an abiding fear of what lingers beyond the grave. Unlike the frightful echoes of modern lore, Greek shades were often tragic, restless remnants bound to the mortal world by unfinished rites or violent ends. The nature of one's death determined the nature of one's afterlife. Warriors fallen in battle might find honor among the wraiths, while the unburied and forgotten drifted in torment between worlds.

Most feared among these spirits were the ataphoi, the unburied dead. Without proper funeral rites, a soul could not cross fully into the kingdom of Hades. Condemned to wander between worlds, these spirits cried out for rest. Even in epic tales, such as the *Iliad*, the shade of Patroclus appears in a dream, begging Achilles for burial, his essence barred from the Underworld until his body was returned to the earth.

Not all souls were mournful. Some retained potency beyond the grave, avengers of broken oaths or protectors of sacred lands. Oracles called upon their whispers, and heroes' spirits were invoked to sway battles. Yet the presence of ghosts also haunted daily life. Crossroads were avoided, thresholds salted, and the festival of Lemuria was held to appease the dead. For the Greeks, the boundary between life and death was not a wall, but a veil—thin, trembling, and always near.

Shadows Between Worlds

The shades of the Underworld were not mere remnants. They were the living memory of the dead, drifting between worlds as reminders of mortality and consequence. Spirits embodied the truth that death was not an end, but a transformation, one that could grant peace, offer wisdom, or condemn the soul to eternal unrest. Whether summoned in sacred rites or feared in the silence of night, the shades endured. They whispered across generations, a solemn echo that no life passes without memory—no death without shadow.

THE TWILIGHT CURTAIN

The kingdom below was not merely the resting place of souls, nor the silent dominion of Hades alone. It was a realm alive with ancient power, populated by deities, spirits, and monstrous sentinels who upheld the laws of death and shadow. These beings did not dwell in darkness as exiles, but as keepers of balance, enforcing the will of the cosmos through fear, mystery, and sacred duty. From the watchful eyes of spectral judges to the monstrous guardians at the gates, each presence shaped the realm into more than a grave—it became a living myth, ruled by silence and twilight.

"There in the depths dwell many a dread form,
Spirits nameless, gods of shadow,
Ruling over the dead with silent power."
— Orphic Hymn to Hades

Guardians of the Gates

At the threshold of the Underworld stood a creature no soul could defy—Cerberus, the hound of Hades, monstrous and unrelenting. With three snarling heads and a mane of writhing serpents, he stood as both sentinel and symbol, a beast forged not for terror, but for order itself. Some said his three heads gazed into the past, present, and future, ensuring no secret passed unnoticed and no transgressor went unseen. Coiled in scales and shadow, he embodied the chthonic realm itself—dreadful, watchful, and absolute.

Though monstrous in size, Cerberus was no mindless beast. He served Hades with unwavering loyalty, guarding the boundary between life and death with dedicated precision. None entered without leave. None departed without doom. Even Heracles, mightiest of mortals, could not subdue the hound by strength alone. Only with Hades' permission did the hero pass, bearing Cerberus into the world above for but a fleeting moment, proof that even the strongest bowed before the laws of death.

Wings of Judgement

The Harpies, daughters of storm and shadow, soared as winged instruments of celestial punishment. With the bodies of birds and faces twisted in rage, they were not monsters, but ordained enforcers of retribution. Their flight was a curse carried on the wind, their arrival a sign that the gods had passed judgment. When mortals defied the natural order or betrayed divine law, it was the Harpies who descended—snatching, tormenting, and dragging souls toward their deserved fate.

Their most infamous victim was King Phineus, cursed for revealing the secrets of the gods. As he reached for food, the Harpies swept down in fury, fouling every meal and leaving him in never-ending hunger until the Boreads, sons of the North Wind, drove them away. Vicious, yet just, these spirits were loathed not for their malice, but for their purpose. They embodied a cosmic truth that vengeance, when born of hallowed order, comes not with mercy, but with wings and storm.

Mother of Shadows and Silence

Nyx, primordial goddess of the night, emerged from the void before the Olympians, her shadow falling across both the living world and the dead. She was the mother of Hypnos, the gentle bringer of sleep, and Thanatos, the silent hand of death—twins who guided mortals from the world of dreams to the threshold of eternity. Nyx moved unseen through the heavens, cloaking creation in stillness, her veil drawn across the eyes of gods and mortals alike.

Even Zeus, wielder of thunder, was said to fear her, such was her ancient power. For Nyx did not command by force, but by inevitability. She embodied the mysteries beyond life's final breath. Sleep that softens the soul, death that silences it. In her, the Greeks saw the vast unknowable night, eternal and sovereign, from which all darkness flows and to which all life must one day return.

Darkness Between Worlds

Erebus, one of the firstborn of creation, was the embodiment of darkness itself. Older than Hades, older even than the Olympians, he filled the chasms of the Underworld with his shadow, veiling the threshold between the living and the dead. His name became a synonym for the gloom that cloaked the soul's descent, a silence so absolute it seemed eternal.

Though Erebus rarely moved within the myths, his presence was constant, an unspoken force that haunted the edges of existence. As consort to Nyx, he helped bring forth the spirits of death, sleep, and fate, tying him to the most sacred transitions of life. Through

Erebus, the Greeks glimpsed the void that waits for all things—a domain not of malice, but of inevitable return.

Torchbearer at the Crossroads

Hecate, goddess of witchcraft and shadowed thresholds, stood as a sovereign of liminal spaces—guardian of the crossroads, keeper of necromantic rites, and companion of the dead. Cloaked in twilight and crowned in flame, she bore torches that pierced the boundary between worlds, guiding lost souls through the gloom of the Underworld. Neither fully of the living nor entirely of the dead, Hecate moved between realms with divine ease.

Feared as much as revered, she presided over spells, omens, and sacred rites. To those who sought prophecy or power from beyond, Hecate offered a path—mystic and perilous. Her worshippers left offerings where roads diverged, calling upon her to grant wisdom or shield them from wandering wraiths. She was no mere enchantress. Hecate was the boundary incarnate, where providence, magic, and death converged.

Keepers of the Veil

In the shadowed depths of the Underworld, the Lampades moved like whispers of flame—torch-bearing nymphs in service to Hecate. Their torches lit the path through shadows, casting ghostly light upon the unseen and guiding those who dared to seek the wisdom of the dead. As companions to the goddess, they walked the margins of the mortal and the divine, illuminating the shroud between worlds with each silent step.

More than attendants of Hecate, the Lampades were spirits of passage and power. In some tales, they led wandering souls to their final rest. In others, they stood sentinel over rites of necromancy and revelation. Their presence marked places of enchantment and danger, where the ordinary world gave way to twilight and silence. Through them, the mysteries of Hecate endured, flame flickering at the edge of the unknown.

Phantoms of Dread

Among the most chilling spirits of the Underworld were the Empusa, phantoms in service to Hecate. These shape-shifting beings haunted lonely crossroads and moonless paths, cloaked in illusion and terror. With one leg of brass and one of beast, they walked between forms, often appearing as radiant maidens to deceive the unwary before revealing their monstrous visage and feasting upon blood and flesh.

Born of nightmare and sorcery, the Empusa were omens of death and madness, their presence a corruption of beauty and a warning of what waits in shadow. They blurred the boundaries between ghost and demon, mortal and monstrous, lingering where the divide was thin and fear was thick. Through whispered tales and restless dreams, their legend endured, specters of desire and dread, still lurking where the mortal world forgets to look.

Ghostlight of the Underworld

Melinoë, the spectral daughter of the Underworld, walked the boundary between sleep and death. A goddess of ghosts, dreams, and haunted memory, she wandered through the veil of night, her form divided—one side luminous as moonlight, the other cloaked in shadow. Born, some say, of Hades and Persephone, she embodied the restless spirits that slipped between worlds, unseen yet ever present.

Unlike the silent gods of judgment or the guardians who barred escape, Melinoë reached into the mortal world, shaping the minds of dreamers with visions of the dead. Her touch stirred nightmares and unearthed forgotten sorrows, reminding the living that the departed were never truly gone. Those who beheld her never woke the same, for her presence revealed the truths that sleep conceals, and her name lingered like a chill in the soul.

Spirits of Violent Death

The Keres soared on wings of shadow—dark spirits drawn to blood's scent and the cry of the dying. Where Thanatos brought silence and repose, the Keres thrived in carnage, descending upon battlefields to seize the souls of those struck down by sword, spear, or rage. Clad in black and crowned with dread, they did not guide souls gently. The Keres tore them from broken bodies, dragging them screaming into the depths of the Underworld.

They were neither gods to be prayed to nor spirits to be bargained with. The Keres were inevitability made flesh, the personification of death's cruelest hand. Feared yet accepted, they haunted the edge of every mortal conflict, a reminder that not all deaths are serene. In their wake lay torn banners, lifeless eyes, and the unburied fallen, testaments to the truth that the kingdom below claims its due in many forms, and war is its most ravenous servant.

Faces in the Dark

The Underworld was not an empty abyss. It was a realm of purpose, haunted by forms both divine and monstrous. Its shadows were shaped by guardians and hunters, by whispering shades and ancient gods, all bound to the eternal task of order beyond the grave. From the burning eyes of Cerberus to the blade-winged descent of the Keres, each being played a part in sustaining the balance between worlds—the veil unbroken, the shadow ever present. They were not dwellers of death, but keepers of fate—woven into the dark fabric of a realm where memory endures, justice is absolute, and no soul crosses without consequence.

SPIRITS OF THE SHROUDED REALM

The Underworld was not merely a realm of judgment and torment; it was a dominion shaped by spirits, beasts, and guardians bound to the sacred law of death. From the relentless Furies who avenged the oath-breaker to Cerberus, the hound with three heads and one will, every being served a single purpose. To preserve the boundary between worlds. Shades passed through ashen meadows, pale echoes of the living, while dread spirits—the Keres, the Empusa—prowled the darker margins, their presence a reminder that even in death, terror endures.

Yet within this world of silence and shadow, the Underworld was more than a prison. It was a mirror. Here, divine order met mortal consequence; here, the soul was seen for what it was. The living who crossed its threshold did so at peril, seeking truth, redemption, or the faces of those lost to time. Some emerged changed, others never rose again.

As we leave behind the guardians and ghosts of Hades' dominion, we follow those who dared to descend—the heroes who defied the will of fate and entered the depths, not to flee death, but to confront it.

CHAPTER 8

CROSSING THE
THRESHOLD

Descent into the Realm of Shadows

Though the gates of Hades were forged for souls, not flesh, a rare few among the living dared to descend. Guided by love, glory, or divine will, mortals braved the realm of shadow in search of what death had claimed. Their paths were fraught with peril—for none crossed into the Underworld unchanged. Whether victorious or lost, their journeys carved timeless myths into the fabric of eternity—marks no mortal hand could erase. To cross that boundary was to barter the living breath for memory itself.

> *"Few among mortals have dared to*
> *tread that shadowed path,*
> *To gaze upon the realm of the dead and return again,*
> *For the gates of Hades are open for all,*
> *but none may leave."*
> — Homer, *Odyssey*

Final Labor of Heracles

Among the final and most fearsome of Heracles' twelve labors was a task that defied the very laws of mortality. To descend into the Underworld and return with Cerberus, the monstrous hound who guarded its gates. Ordered by the fearful King Eurystheus, this labor demanded more than strength. It required a mortal to brave the shadows of death, to walk the land of shades and emerge alive. Heracles would not only face the beast, but also win the favor of Hades and Persephone, gods not easily swayed.

Through the gloom of the kingdom below, he encountered restless souls, including Meleager, who urged him to protect his sister Deianira. Pressing onward, he stood before the thrones of the dead and received Hades' grim bargain. Heracles could take Cerberus only if he subdued the beast without weapons. Unarmed yet undeterred, he wrestled the serpent-maned guardian, enduring its fury until at last it yielded.

When Heracles emerged, dragging Cerberus into the light of the living, it was not just a triumph of strength, it was a defiance of death itself. Yet no one enters the depths of the dead unchanged. In conquering the veiled depths most fearsome sentinel, Heracles returned not simply as a hero, but as one who had glimpsed the end of all things—and returned bearing its shadow.

Song That Broke the Silence

Orpheus did not descend into the dark abyss by command or conquest, but by the aching pull of love undone. When Eurydice, his bride, perished from a serpent's bite on their wedding day, grief carved a hollow in his soul that no earthly music could fill. Armed with his lyre and a voice woven from sorrow, Orpheus entered the kingdom of Hades, his melodies softening the hearts of even the deathless.

Before the thrones of Hades and Persephone, he played—not with power, but with pure longing. The gods were moved. They granted him a single, fragile hope. Eurydice would follow him back, silent and unseen, so long as he did not turn to gaze upon her until both had returned to the light.

Through dim corridors and ash-pale paths, he led, her footsteps an echo behind him. But just before the final threshold, fear stole his faith. He turned.

And she vanished.

Not slain, not stolen, but reclaimed by the laws he could not confront. The tragedy of Orpheus was not failure of love, but of trust, a human flaw magnified by divine conditions. In life, he wandered alone, his music haunted by what might have been. In death, Orpheus joined her, beyond song, beyond sorrow.

Hubris of Theseus and Pirithous

Not all who descended into the depths of the dead were guided by love or bound by serendipity. Some came with pride in their hearts and ambition in their steps—and none more so than Theseus and Pirithous. Warriors of renown, they believed their deeds had earned them divine brides. After abducting Helen of Sparta for Theseus, their gaze turned to a greater, forbidden prize. Persephone, queen of the dead.

With reckless confidence, they entered the depths below, intent on seizing the bride of Hades himself. But the Underworld does not yield to mortal will. As they sat upon a massive stone throne in Hades' palace, invisible bonds tightened around them. The throne became their snare, and the kingdom their prison, ensnared not by force, but by the weight of their hubris.

For daring to steal from death, they were condemned to stillness and silence, trapped in the depths of the Underworld for eternity. Only Theseus would later be spared, rescued by Heracles through celestial petition. Pirithous remained behind, bound forever in shadow, a monument to the peril of mortal arrogance before divine law.

Toll of Descent

Each hero who dared descend into the domain of the dead did so under a different star—love, duty, vengeance, or reckless pride.

Yet all who crossed the threshold met one truth. The Underworld tests not strength alone, but spirit. In its depths, even the mighty are laid bare. Some emerged triumphant, others shattered. None returned unchanged.

Their journeys became immortal echoes—tales whispered by poets, etched into marble, and passed from oracle to child. They serve as both warning and wonder that the land of the dead is no place for the living, and those who trespass upon its silence carry its shadow forever—proof that even victory leaves a toll unpaid.

MORTAL DESCENT

Few tales stir the soul like those of mortals who braved the Underworld—and lived to tell of it. Compelled by love, honor, or the summons of fate, they crossed into Hades' domain, where breath fades, judgment reigns, and the sun dares not shine. These journeys carved timeless myths, proof that even in the heart of death, the living will could still echo loud enough to reach the gods.

> "Not by strength nor by might does one return from Hades,
> But by the will of the gods alone may a soul be restored
> From the land where the sun's light never reaches."
> — Euripides, *Alcestis*

A Hero Among Ghosts

Among the many trials endured by Odysseus, none proved more haunting than his communion with the dead. In Homer's *Odyssey*, the hero does not descend fully into Hades but instead performs a sacred rite at the edge of the world, summoning the silent shades through an act of necromancy. Guided by Circe's counsel, Odysseus seeks the wisdom of the blind prophet Tiresias, whose voice alone can illuminate the path home.

In the mist-wrapped land of the Cimmerians, where no sun ever shines, Odysseus carves a trench into the earth, filling it with libations of milk, honey, dark wine, and the blood of a sacrificial ram. Attracted by the scent of life, the dead rose from their silence, ghosts drifted forth in mournful procession. First comes Elpenor, his fallen comrade, begging for burial so his soul may rest. Then appear the shades of mighty warriors—Achilles, Agamemnon, and others—each bearing the mark of their sorrow, their once-glorious deeds now reduced to ash and memory.

When Tiresias emerges, the air stills. The prophet spoke a truth carved by fate, "Odysseus shall return, but only through suffering." He warns of Poseidon's wrath and pleads restraint with the sacred cattle of Helios. And then, with chilling clarity, he offers a final vision, not of war or renown, but of a distant journey inland, where Odysseus must plant an oar in the earth and make peace with the sea god one last time.

This vision of the dead is no mere episode of adventure. It is a solemn unveiling. Odysseus sees what lies beyond valor that even the greatest heroes fade, that death grants no favor, and that only wisdom, earned through hardship, may shield a soul from the relentless hand of fate. Odysseus did not descend for conquest, but for clarity.

The Bough of Fate

While Odysseus sought the counsel of the dead to secure his homecoming, Aeneas, heir of Troy and vessel of fate, descended into the Underworld to glimpse the divine tapestry of Rome's future. His was no mortal errand, but a sacred passage, an ordeal ordained by the gods to affirm the destiny of a new world.

Led by the Sibyl of Cumae, he ventured to Lake Avernus, where the boundary between life and death grew thin. There, he secured the golden bough, an ethereal token demanded by the chthonic gods, granting him passage into the land of shadows. Beyond the gates, Aeneas beheld a dominion of sorrow and wonder, where grief and glory walked hand in hand.

In the Fields of Mourning, he found Queen Dido, silent in death as she had been passionate in life. Her ghost turned away, a wound of love left unhealed, reminding Aeneas of the cost of divine obedience. Deeper still, he walked the halls of judgment, where souls were weighed and fates decreed. The wicked fell into Tartarus, while the virtuous ascended to the Elysian Fields, eternal meadows for those who walked in honor.

At last, he stood before his father, Anchises, who unveiled the visions of a mighty empire yet to rise. In that revelation, Aeneas understood that his trials were not his own, but offerings to destiny itself. Unlike Odysseus, who returned burdened by mortality, Aeneas emerged from the Underworld renewed—his soul tempered by sacrifice, his path sanctified by the echoes of those who came before.

Trial of the Soul

Unlike the warriors who braved the Underworld for prophecy or glory, Psyche entered the realm of the dead not with sword or lyre, but with love as her guide and suffering as her companion. In the tale told by Apuleius, Psyche's descent was not of conquest, but of endurance, humility, and divine awakening.

Psyche, a mortal of extraordinary beauty, had captured the heart of Eros, god of desire. Yet, through jealousy and trials set by Aphrodite, she found herself cast into despair, separated from the god she loved. To prove her devotion, she was commanded to undertake impossible labors, the final of which required her to descend into the Underworld and retrieve a fragment of Persephone's beauty, sealed within a box of shadowed power.

Guided by whispered counsel, Psyche followed the path of the dead. She journeyed past the boundaries of the living, encountered Charon and his mournful ferry, and offered him the toll of the dead. She stilled the hunger of Cerberus with honeyed cakes, passing unharmed into Hades' somber halls. There, in the throne room of Persephone, Psyche humbly made her request. The queen, moved by her sincerity, placed the box in her hands and permitted her return.

But as Psyche ascended, mortal temptation took hold. Believing she could claim a measure of divine beauty, she opened the box, only to fall into a deathlike sleep. It was not willpower that saved her, but love. Eros, seeing her lifeless form, revived her with a touch. Carried to Olympus, Psyche was granted immortality by Zeus himself, her trials fulfilled, her soul eternal.

Psyche's descent was not marked by heroic conquest, but by the quiet strength of devotion. In facing death without weapon or wrath, she emerged not merely alive, but divine.

Path to Transformation

The Underworld is a realm forbidden to the living, yet three mortals—Odysseus, Aeneas, and Psyche—braved its darkened depths and returned forever altered. Odysseus beheld the pale silence of the dead and came to know the weight of fate and the frailty of mortal strength. Aeneas walked among the shades of heroes and tyrants, emerging with divine purpose etched upon his soul. Psyche, led not by valor but by love, descended as a mortal and rose immortal, her spirit tempered by trials no god could ignore.

These tales endure not merely as myths, but as eternal truths that to pass through darkness is to be remade by it—that the descent into the shadow is the first step toward transformation, illumination, and the birth of something greater than before.

WISDOM FROM THE DEPTHS

The tales of those who braved the Underworld and returned are not merely sagas of peril. They are mirrors held to the soul of humankind. Beneath their mythic grandeur lies a deeper revelation that to descend into darkness is to awaken to truth. Each mortal, whether hero, wanderer, or lover, faced the abyss and emerged transformed, bearing insight etched by shadow. These myths endure as sacred allegories, exploring the perils of forbidden knowledge, the trials of inner reckoning, and the eternal cycle of death, renewal, and cosmic remembrance.

"Blessed is he who has seen these things
before he goes beneath the earth;
for he understands the end of mortal life,
and he knows its god-given beginning."
— Homeric Hymn to Demeter

Crucible of the Dead

In Greek mythology, the Underworld was not merely a realm of the dead. It was a threshold of profound change. To cross into Hades' domain was to step beyond the known world, into a realm where mortality dissolved and deeper truths were laid bare. The laws of this realm governed not the body, but the soul, reflecting the inner trials of those who dared to enter.

For Odysseus, the journey marked a passage of reckoning. Among the shades of fallen warriors, he glimpsed the fragile echo of glory. Even mighty Achilles, once unmatched in battle, lamented the cold silence of death. This encounter shattered the illusion of heroism and prepared Odysseus to return not as a conqueror, but as one tempered by loss and humility.

Aeneas, by contrast, descended not for himself, but for the destiny of a people. Guided by divine will, his vision within the Underworld revealed Rome's future splendor, and the sacrifices it demanded. There, amid the fields of sorrow and of judgment, he shed his uncertainty. He emerged no longer a wandering exile, but a bearer of fate, sanctified by purpose.

Psyche entered the abyss below not as a warrior, but as a mortal in search of love. Her journey was one of faith and endurance. Unlike the heroes before her, she was not seeking power or prophecy, but redemption through devotion. Her trials tested the spirit, not the sword, and in passing through them, she transcended death itself. Psyche's rebirth into divinity proved that even the most fragile heart could endure the shadows and rise immortal.

Each tale reveals that the Underworld was never a terminus, but a crucible. Those who crossed its threshold—whether gods, heroes, or mortals—faced the deepest truths of existence. And though they returned to the world above, they did so altered, carrying the fire of transformation in their souls.

Price of the Journey

To cross into the Underworld was no casual feat. Even the boldest heroes approached its gates with dread, for the kingdom of Hades exacted a cost from all who entered, and few ever returned. In myth, the journey was never without peril, and the warnings echo still, some who sought the dead lost more than they bargained for.

Among the gravest dangers was the loss of identity. For the departed, this was literal. Souls who drank from the River Lethe surrendered their memories, drifting in silence through the Asphodel Meadows, stripped of name, purpose, and past. For the living, forgetfulness took subtler forms. The sorrow, wonder, and terror of the dark abyss could fracture the self, unmaking even the strongest. Orpheus, blessed with the chance to reclaim Eurydice, faltered in a moment of doubt. One glance back, one lapse in faith—and she was lost. His tragedy teaches that trust, once broken, cannot always be repaired.

Equally dangerous was defying the laws that governed the dead. The world below was sacred, bound by celestial rule. None who entered, mortal or spirit, were meant to leave unbidden. Theseus and Pirithous, who dared to steal Persephone from her throne, found themselves shackled for eternity. Even Heracles, a son of Zeus, required Hades' consent before he could lead Cerberus to the mortal world above. In Hades' domain, strength alone could not guarantee survival, only reverence and restraint.

The silent kingdom was also a labyrinth of half-truths. Specters spoke in riddles, and not all who offered guidance could be trusted.

Aeneas was shielded by the Sibyl's wisdom, her presence a lamp in the darkness. But many who descended alone found themselves lost, wandering paths that turned back upon themselves. In such stories, the Underworld became not just a place, but a test of discernment.

Yet amid these dangers lay a singular gift—knowledge. Those who endured returned with their hearts reshaped. They had looked upon the shadow that awaits all mortals, and in doing so, gained clarity. The myths remind us that the greatest wisdom often lies buried in darkness, and that transformation is born not in triumph, but in trials.

The Sacred Cycle

Among the oldest truths carried through the Underworld myths is the sacred cycle of death and rebirth. In Greek thought, as in many faiths and philosophies, the descent into darkness is not final, but necessary; a passage not into oblivion, but into renewal.

Foremost among these stories is the tale of Persephone, whose abduction by Hades and return to the upper world reflects the rhythm of the seasons. Her journey mirrors the Earth's slumber in winter and its awakening in spring, a divine pattern that reveals death not as an end, but a threshold to transformation.

So too did heroes undergo symbolic deaths in their travels through Hades' domain. Odysseus, as he spoke with the dead, came face to face with his own mortality, and saw that even Achilles—once the greatest of warriors—now longed for the light of life. Aeneas, witnessing souls poised for rebirth, understood the cosmic design that bound past, present, and future together, and emerged with a divine purpose forged in shadow. Psyche, cast into a deathless sleep by the contents of Persephone's box, was ultimately awakened not as a mortal, but as a goddess—her suffering a crucible that transfigured her spirit.

These myths echo beyond their time, shaping the mysteries of religion and philosophy alike. Countless traditions hold that the soul descends—must break, surrender, and suffer—before it can be made whole. Whether in baptism, initiation, or the turning of the Earth itself, Greek mythology planted a lasting truth; before one can rise, one must pass through darkness.

The Fire That Endures

The tales of those who braved the Underworld and returned speak not only of peril and sorrow, but of the soul's capacity for transformation. The realm of the dead was never solely a place of endings, but a crucible of change, where mortals were tested and their true nature revealed. Each descent confronted the traveler with echoes of temptation, loss, and hubris, warning against the defiance of divine law. Yet those who endured emerged with deeper wisdom, forever shaped by what they had seen. At the heart of every myth lay a sacred truth. Death is not always a conclusion, but a passage, one that promises renewal, if one can withstand the darkness. Even in the deepest vaults of Hades, the flame of rebirth endures.

THROUGH SHADOW, TOWARD LIGHT

The Underworld, realm of the dead, was nonetheless crossed by the living—heroes who defied its silence in pursuit of love, truth, or destiny. Each journey pressed the limits of human endurance, revealing divine law and the soul's inescapable trials. Odysseus returned with the burden of wisdom, Aeneas with the weight of fate, Orpheus with the ache of irreversible loss, and Heracles with the scars of triumph. None emerged unaltered. Their tales endure as sacred echoes, reminding us that within darkness lies the seed of transformation.

Yet Hades' realm held more than challenge and sorrow. It guarded mysteries meant not for conquest, but for communion. Beneath its shrouds of silence lay sacred knowledge, guarded by rites and initiations that offered mortals a glimpse beyond the veil. The next descent is not with swords or sorrow, but in reverence, to explore the Eleusinian Mysteries, where Persephone's descent became the symbol of return, renewal, and the soul's awakening beyond death.

CHAPTER 9

RETURN AND
REVELATION

Flame of the Eleusinian Mysteries

Shrouded in silence and guarded by oaths older than memory, the Eleusinian Mysteries formed the heart of ancient Greek spirituality. Concealed within temple walls and passed only through initiation, these rites—devoted to Demeter and Persephone—offered not ceremony, but revelation. They promised a vision of the soul's journey through death and into blessed renewal, a truth glimpsed only by the chosen few. Though much of their detail is lost to time, the remnants that remain speak of a consecrated drama, one that shaped myth, philosophy, and the very hope of immortality for generations to come.

> *"Happy is he among men upon earth*
> *who has seen these mysteries;*
> *but he who is uninitiated and has no part in them*
> *never has the same lot once dead in the dreary darkness."*
> — *Homeric Hymn to Demeter*

Seeds of the Sacred

The roots of the Eleusinian Mysteries reached deep into the sorrow of a grieving mother and the turning of the seasons. When Persephone was taken by Hades into the Underworld, Demeter wandered the earth in anguish. Cloaked as an aged woman, she came to Eleusis, where the mortal King Celeus and Queen Metaneira received her in kindness.

To repay their compassion, Demeter sought to bless their infant son, Demophon, with immortality, using an ancient rite of fire and ambrosia. But when Metaneira interrupted the act in fear, the goddess revealed her divine form, radiant and terrible. Her mourning became revelation. Demeter commanded that a great temple be raised in her honor, and within its stone walls she taught mortals the hallowed rites that would echo through a thousand years, the Mysteries of Eleusis, born not of conquest but of compassion.

At the heart of these rites lay the story of loss and return. As Demeter withdrew her gifts of grain and harvest from the earth, famine spread and mortals despaired. Only when Persephone was allowed to rise again for part of each year did the world awaken. Thus were born the seasons, and with them, the sacred truth that life and death are not opposites, but eternal companions.

The initiates who entered Demeter's sanctuary did not merely hear this myth. They lived it. Through ritual and silence, they shared in the goddess's grief, her descent into darkness, and the joy of her daughter's return. What began as mourning became a promise that from sorrow may come renewal, and from death, divine understanding.

Hidden Visions

Though the Eleusinian Mysteries stood at the spiritual heart of Greece, their inner truth remained forever veiled. Those who crossed the sacred threshold took an oath of silence so absolute that to betray it meant death. Unlike other rites sung in verse or carved in stone, these ceremonies left no scripture, only the memory of revelation. They were not a doctrine to be taught, but an experience to be lived—wordless, transformative, divine.

From fragments and whispers, we glimpse the path of initiation. The seekers fasted, purified themselves in the sea, and joined a moonlit procession from Athens to Eleusis, torches flickering like souls in passage. Within the Telesterion, the great hall of mysteries, they beheld a sacred drama. Demeter's grief, Persephone's return, and the triumph of life over death. In that moment of epopteia—the vision—light pierced the darkness, and the mortal heart glimpsed eternity.

What was revealed cannot be known. Some spoke of a sheaf of grain raised aloft, others of a sudden blaze, or the taste of kykeon, an ancient Greek drink, that bridged worlds. Yet all who emerged from the ritual spoke of a serenity beyond fear. The Mysteries did not teach. They awakened.

The greatest minds of Greece revered this awakening. Plato likened it to the soul's ascent from shadow into truth. Pindar called those who beheld it "blessed among mortals." Cicero wrote that it gave life meaning and death no sting. Though the fires of Eleusis have long since faded, their light endures—within every search for what lies beyond the veil.

LIGHT BEYOND THE SHADOWS

The Eleusinian Mysteries stood as a bridge between worlds, where light touched darkness, and mortality brushed the edge of the divine. Within the silent halls of Eleusis, torchlight flickered like captured dawn, illuminating truths that language could not hold. To those who entered, the veil between life and death grew thin, and what had seemed shadow revealed its hidden radiance. The rites spoke of renewal through descent, of wisdom earned through silence, and of the soul's awakening through suffering. In that sacred dimness, mortals glimpsed eternity—not as an end, but as a return to the light that had always awaited them.

"Blessed is he who has beheld these sacred rites,
for he shall know the end of life and its god-sent beginning. "
— Pindar, *Fragment*

Silence of the Initiate

From the moment an initiate took the solemn oath of Eleusis, they became bound not merely by tradition, but by ordained covenant. This vow of silence was no ordinary pledge. It was a sanctified obligation, upheld by fear of cosmic retribution. So revered were the ceremonies that even philosophers, poets, and playwrights spoke of them only in veiled allusion. To betray the rites was to court exile, dishonor, or death, for what had been revealed within the hallowed sanctuary of Eleusis was not meant for the uninitiated ear.

Yet what hallowed purpose lay in such secrecy. The answer dwelled not in doctrine, but in revelation, an experience to be lived, not taught. The initiates walked a sanctified path mirroring the descent and return of Demeter and Persephone. To reveal its mystery was to profane its sanctity and unravel its power.

And beyond the spiritual gravity lay another truth. The rites of Eleusis offered a form of inner knowing set apart from all other rites. While most Greek ceremonies were communal and public, Eleusis conferred a private grace, a hallowed wisdom accessible only to those chosen to receive it. In that secrecy dwelled both its majesty and its endurance—for over a thousand years, the ceremonies of Eleusis stood inviolate, not by force, but by awe.

Call to the Worthy

Though kept in secrecy, the Eleusinian Mysteries were remarkably inclusive in spirit, welcoming a far broader fellowship than most holy rites of the ancient world. Unlike the closed circles of aristocratic priesthoods, the path to Eleusis lay open to all freeborn Greeks, whether plowmen or kings, so long as they had not stained their hands with blood. Over time, even the so-called barbarians, strangers to Hellenic lands and tongue, were permitted to tread the sacred road, provided they could speak the language and had lived justly.

Yet not all were deemed worthy. Slaves, whose lives were not their own, were excluded. Not from cruelty, but from a belief that only those with freedom of will could truly walk the transformative path. Likewise, those who had committed grave crimes, especially murder, were denied entry, for the Mysteries demanded purity not of birth, but of soul. The journey into the sanctified required a heart unburdened by unspeakable guilt.

Among the initiates stood emperors and sages. Even Marcus Aurelius, philosopher-king of Rome, sought the rites of Eleusis, centuries after the classical age had waned. His presence among the initiated testified to the reach of the practice, which transcended city, nation, and empire. For those who longed to understand life's end and its celestial beginning, Eleusis offered not exclusion, but eternal invitation.

Blessed Fate Beyond

Among all the gifts bestowed by the Eleusinian Mysteries, none was greater than the promise that death was not an end, but a threshold. In the traditional vision held by the ancient Greeks, the afterlife loomed as a pale and joyless realm. Most souls, stripped of memory and meaning, wandered the mist-veiled Asphodel Meadows, neither punished nor rewarded, but consigned to forgetful drift. Only heroes, and those whom the gods cherished, might ascend to the Elysian Fields, basking in light beyond sorrow.

Yet the practice reimagined this destiny. For those initiated into the spiritual rites, a new vision of the afterlife took shape—one luminous, hopeful, and serene. Though the exact nature of this blessed world remained forever unspoken, cloaked in the vow of silence, ancient voices hint at its splendor. It was believed that the rites conferred godly favor, guiding the soul to a gentler resting place, far from the colorless monotony of Asphodel.

Great minds bore witness to this truth. Pindar, the poet, declared that those who had beheld the sacred vision would know joy after death, dwelling in radiant meadows untouched by grief. Cicero, the philosopher-statesman, spoke of the Mysteries as a light that banished the fear of dying. To walk the ordained path of Eleusis was to be reborn in spirit, gifted with a tranquil certainty that the soul endured, and flourished, beyond the veil.

At the heart of this hope lay the myth of Demeter and Persephone. As Persephone journeyed each year into the darkness and rose again into the living world, so too might the soul fall into death and rise once more into light. The cycle of loss and return, of descent and rebirth, offered more than seasonal symbolism. It offered salvation. Later rites and religions, from Orphism to the early Christian mysteries, echoed this sacred rhythm.

Though the inner truths of Eleusis remain sealed in silence, one legacy endures with certainty. The Mysteries reshaped how the Greeks understood death. What had once been a grim inevitability became a path toward peace, a passage not into oblivion, but into something blessed. The souls who stepped into the Telesterion emerged transformed, no longer fearing the end, but believing in the eternal.

Echoes of Eleusis

The Eleusinian Mysteries were more than rituals. They were a path to transformation. Cloaked in sacred silence, they preserved their power by granting revelation only to those who truly sought it. By opening their sanctuary to all freeborn Greeks, regardless of station, they forged a spiritual tradition that transcended class and city. And by offering the promise of a blessed afterlife, they reshaped the Greek vision of death—replacing shadow with radiance, despair with hope. The Mysteries cast their light far beyond the hallowed halls of Eleusis, influencing the ancient world's deepest questions about life, mortality, and what lies beyond. Though the practice has long faded, the legacy endures— timeless, veiled in mystery, echoing with the footsteps of those who dared to seek.

SACRAMENTS OF THE UNDERWORLD

The bond between Hades and Persephone was more than a tale passed down through myth. It was bound into the sacred order of Greek belief. As sovereigns of the Underworld, they were venerated through solemn rites and whispered prayers, ceremonies meant to honor the gods of the dead and secure harmony between the worlds of the living and the departed. Mystery cults centered their teachings on Persephone's descent and return, offering initiates hidden truths and the promise of salvation beyond the grave. Their story echoed far beyond Eleusis. Philosophers like

Plato drew upon their myth to explore the soul's immortal journey, and later spiritual traditions absorbed their symbols, shaping new visions of death, rebirth, and reunion.

> *"Mighty and revered are Persephone and Hades,*
> *Rulers of souls in the silent halls,*
> *To them the pious offer sacred rites,*
> *Seeking favor in life and peace in death."*
> — *Orphic Hymn to Persephone*

Offerings to the Silent Gods

Among the Olympians, none commanded such reverence as Hades, nor embodied such sacred duality as Persephone. Their worship, unlike that of the sky-bound gods, was conducted not in grandeur but in shadow—marked by silence, secrecy, and the trembling awe of those who sought favor in the face of death.

Hades received no towering temples crowned in sunlight. His name was seldom spoken aloud, and offerings made in his honor followed the ancient rites of the chthonic tradition. Sacrifices were buried in the earth—black rams or other dark-hued animals—given not in spectacle, but in silence. Prayers to Hades were whispered into the ground, as if to speak too boldly might summon his gaze. And yet, he was essential. In funeral rites and tomb inscriptions, in the quiet invocation of his name at the edge of life, Hades was honored as the unyielding guardian of the soul's final passage.

By contrast, Persephone was celebrated with more visible devotion. As queen of the Underworld and harbinger of spring, she stood at the threshold of life and death. Her worship unified the sorrow of loss with the promise of renewal. Festivals in her name, most notably the Eleusinian Mysteries, portrayed her sacred journey into the depths and back to the realm of the living. Through Persephone, the Greek people found hope. She softened the stern decrees of the Underworld, offering mercy where only judgment might have stood.

Together, Hades and Persephone formed a divine axis between mortality and immortality. To honor them was not to seek favor, but to walk with reverence between worlds. Their rites reminded mortals of a truth both terrifying and profound Death is not only an end, but a gate, and that beyond its silence may lie the grace of return.

Rites of Transcendence

Mystery cults held a sacred place in the spiritual life of Greece, shaping how mortals understood death, the soul, and the hope of renewal. At the heart of these secret traditions stood Persephone, whose passage between worlds offered a divine model for transcendence.

The Eleusinian Mysteries invited initiates not to witness, but to experience transformation. Through symbolic death and rebirth, they re-enacted Persephone's descent into darkness and her radiant return. It was a journey inward as much as sacred, a revelation achieved not through doctrine, but through divine encounter.

The Orphic tradition deepened this path. Rooted in the songs of Orpheus, it taught that the soul was bound to the cycle of mortal existence, seeking release through purity and remembrance. Persephone, in these rites, was not merely queen of the dead but a liberator, one who opened the way to the Elysian Fields, where the awakened soul might dwell in eternal peace.

Together, these Mysteries offered a sacred alternative to despair. Death was not erasure, but passage; the soul, like the seed in winter, would rise again in light.

Truth Within the Realm

While the Mysteries revealed truth through vision, philosophy sought it through thought. In place of sacred silence, the philosophers offered inquiry—and yet, their questions often echoed the same divine pattern.

Plato, in his *Republic,* spoke of the soul's judgment and rebirth, mirroring the hidden wisdom of Eleusis. In *Phaedo,* he portrayed philosophy itself as initiation, a purification through knowledge, preparing the spirit for its release from the mortal world. The philosopher's task became not unlike that of the initiate—to remember what the soul had once known, to ascend from shadow into light.

In this vision, Hades was transformed. No longer a realm of silence alone, it became the theater of moral truth, where the soul confronted the reflection of its own choices. Death was not a punishment, but a revelation. Through Plato's lens, the myths of the Underworld were reborn as philosophy—carrying the same promise, that wisdom is the path to immortality.

Resonance Through Eternity

Though the sacred fires of Eleusis have long since dimmed, their spirit endures, alive in the human quest for meaning. The rites of Demeter and Persephone, veiled in silence and rich with symbol, seeded ideas that outlived the gods themselves.

In the dawn of Christianity, the same rhythm of descent and return found new form—the divine entering death and rising in renewal. The promise of salvation through suffering, of life restored through love, echoed the path once traced in the Mysteries. The torchlight of Eleusis became the lamp of faith.

Yet the resonance of those rites reaches farther still. Dante's infernal descent, the moral visions of Plato, the secret vows of mystics and seekers—all bear the imprint of that ancient flame. Even now, in the modern soul's hunger for transcendence, we hear its whisper, that death is not an end, but a turning of the wheel toward light.

The Mysteries endure not as ceremony, but as consciousness— a memory within humanity itself, reminding us that every darkness holds the shape of awakening.

Thrones Beyond Time

Hades and Persephone reigned not only over the silent halls of the dead but over the sacred imagination of an entire civilization. In myth and ritual, their presence shaped how mortals conceived the passage from life to afterlife—and what, if anything, lay beyond. Through whispered rites, veiled teachings, and philosophical wonder, their influence reached far beyond temple walls, embedding itself in the soul's search for meaning.

Mystery cults offered salvation through their names. Philosophers like Plato contemplated the soul's return, inspired by the cycles they embodied. And as later religions rose upon new altars, they carried echoes of Eleusis, adopting its themes of descent, suffering, renewal, and divine reunion.

The sacred groves are now overgrown, and the stone foundations of Eleusis lie open to the sun, but the truths once guarded in silence still stir beneath the surface of human belief. The tale of Hades and Persephone, eternal rulers of the realm below, endures not only in memory but in every question humanity asks of death, rebirth, and possibility of grace.

ILLUMINATION IN THE AGE OF MYTH

In the twilight of Greece's sacred age, the Eleusinian Mysteries shone as a living flame of revelation, a light that bridged myth and philosophy, faith and eternity. Within their veiled ceremonies, mortals glimpsed a truth older than temples, that divinity was not distant, but cyclical, reflected in death and renewal. The rites of Demeter and Persephone transformed myth from memory into experience, awakening the soul to its own eternal rhythm. As these mysteries rippled outward through time, they became more than ritual. They became a mirror through which the Greeks, and all who followed, sought to understand the passage of the soul, the purpose of suffering, and the promise of rebirth.

"Wonderful indeed is the mystery revealed among men;
happy is he who has beheld it,
for he knows the end and purpose of life."
— Sophocles, *Fragment*

Path to Elysium

In an age when the next world loomed in shadow, the Eleusinian Mysteries offered a rare and radiant promise, a path beyond the gloom, toward peace, renewal, and divine favor. The common belief among the Greeks held that, after death, most souls drifted into the gray meadows of Asphodel, stripped of joy and memory. Elysium, that luminous paradise of heroes and the virtuous few, seemed a reward too distant for the ordinary mortal. But Eleusis unveiled another vision that salvation was not the privilege of demigods alone, but a gift offered to those who sought initiation.

Within the sacred rites, the myth of Demeter and Persephone pulsed with symbolic power. Demeter's descent into sorrow at the loss of her daughter, and their eventual reunion, became the divine mirror of human grief and hope. Just as the goddess mourned in winter and rejoiced in spring, so too did the Mysteries teach that death was but a season, that beyond the silence of the grave, the soul could bloom again. Though the full nature of the rituals remains veiled in secrecy, many believed the initiate was led through death's shadow and into awakening, echoing Persephone's cycle between darkness and light.

To pass through the Mysteries was to confront mortality with courage and come away transformed. It was to glimpse, if only for a moment, the eternal pattern that governed all life, that every descent held within it the promise of ascent. In offering this vision, the Eleusinian Mysteries redefined death itself, not as an end, but as a sacred threshold. Their message endures still. In embracing the mysteries, one may find not dread, but destiny.

From Lore to Revelation

The Eleusinian Mysteries were more than rites of devotion. They transformed myth itself, turning lore into living revelation. Before Eleusis, myth stood apart—distant lore explaining the gods, not embodying them. But within the sacred walls of the Mysteries, myth became personal. It transformed from tale into ritual, from narrative into lived revelation. The descent of Persephone reflected the initiate's own journey through death, transformation, and rebirth.

This mythic shift reverberated across Greek thought, changing the way myths were told, interpreted, and embodied. The tale of Persephone's abduction, her time among the dead, and her radiant return became more than allegory. It grew into a template for the soul's pilgrimage through mortality. The rites at Eleusis invited Greeks to enter that story not as a listener, but as a participant, one who could mirror the path of hallowed descent and restoration.

In this sacred retelling, myth and philosophy intertwined. The Orphic Mysteries expanded upon the Eleusinian message, teaching that the soul was ensnared in a cycle of reincarnation, its liberation dependent on moral and spiritual purification. The soul, guided by Persephone and the hidden knowledge of the practice, could transcend the bleak monotony of Asphodel and seek the light of the Elysian Fields. Here, rebirth was not a metaphor but a sacred promise, earned through wisdom, ritual, and remembrance.

Philosophers such as Plato absorbed these truths into the very marrow of their teachings. In *The Republic* and *Phaedo*, he spoke of the soul's immortality, of knowledge as divine recollection, and of the philosopher's path as a kind of initiation. These were not mere abstractions. They echoed the Eleusinian belief that sacred understanding reshaped destiny. In this new vision, myth did not end with the tale, it led the soul toward truth.

Even as centuries passed and the gods of Greece merged with Roman thought, the rites of Eleusis endured. Persephone, reimagined as Proserpina, still traveled between realms. Her story retained its ritual power—seasonal, spiritual, eternal. Through her myth, the legacy of Eleusis flowed into Orphic chants, Platonic dialogues, and Christian gospels alike.

The Immortal Thread

The Eleusinian Mysteries transcended the twilight of ancient Greece. Their sacred ideals took root in later spiritual traditions, flowering most visibly within early Christianity. While the Christian path to salvation diverged in doctrine, its central promise of resurrection and triumph over death bore a striking resemblance to the Eleusinian vision of rebirth. The sacred journey of initiation, the transmission of hidden knowledge, and the hope of eternal joy were not new. They echoed the footsteps once taken through the shadowed halls of Eleusis.

Even in the modern age, the breath of Eleusis still stirs beneath the world's silence. It lingers in the pages of literature, in the strokes of art, and in the whispered doctrines of contemporary spirituality. The concept of a concealed truth, one that unveils deeper understanding to the worthy, finds its origin in the Mysteries. From the hidden orders of mystics to the whispered creeds of modern seekers, all owe a silent debt to the torchbearers of Demeter and Persephone. The mythic arc of descent into darkness followed by a luminous return—now a common motif in novels, cinema, and sacred texts—mimics the ritual path once walked by the initiates of Eleusis.

The true power of the Eleusinian Mysteries lies not merely in what they revealed, but in how they endured. They reshaped the human view of mortality, instilling hope where there had once been only fear. In myth, in thought, and in faith, they sowed seeds of wonder that continue to bloom. Though the Telesterion stands in ruins, the vision it housed remains eternal, a flame passed through generations, whispering that beyond death lies not oblivion, but awakening.

A LIGHT CARRIED FORWARD

The Eleusinian Mysteries were not rites to be performed, but revelations to live. Cloaked in silence and veiled from the uninitiated, these hallowed ceremonies opened a gateway to transformation. Through the myth of Demeter and Persephone, the Mysteries sparked a flame of hope amid the shadows of mortality. They taught that from sorrow could rise renewal, and from death, a deeper kind of life. For those who passed through their sacred trials, the promise was clear—not oblivion, but awakening; not silence, but serenity beyond the grave.

Though the marble halls of Eleusis have crumbled and the torches of initiation have long since dimmed, their influence endures. In myth, in philosophy, in the whispered patterns of later religions, the spirit of the rites of Eleusis persists. They left behind no written creed, only echoes carved into the human longing to believe that consciousness journeys onward, guided not by fate alone, but by the sacred light of understanding.

And yet, even as the Mysteries promised transcendence, the Greeks knew the path of every mortal was not their own to walk. Ahead, we turn to the inescapable thread of fate and the voices that foretold it—the Moirai, who spun life's course, and the oracles who gave voice to the divine. For in the ancient world, destiny was not a choice but a decree, etched in shadow, bound in prophecy, and delivered in riddles by those who spoke the will of the gods.

CHAPTER 10

FATE AND
PROPHECY

Clotho, Lachesis, and Atropos

Before gods or mortals took breath, the cosmic loom had already begun to turn, its threads drawn in silence by unseen hands. Fate, to the Greeks, was no decree of Zeus but a power older than Olympus, a rhythm etched into existence itself. Even the gods moved within its pattern. The Moirai, veiled and eternal, guarded this mystery. Clotho spun the thread of life, Lachesis measured its course, and Atropos, with unerring resolve, cut it when the end drew near. No offering could alter their design. In their still labor, the Greeks discerned necessity itself—neither cruel nor merciful, but absolute.

> *"To the Moirai, even the gods must bow,*
> *For their thread is spun, measured, and cut,*
> *And none may escape the fate they weave."*
> — Hesiod, *Theogony*

Weavers of Destiny

Among the eldest powers of creation stood the Moirai—the three weavers of existence who governed the measure of all things born and dying. They were neither merciful nor cruel, neither gods nor servants, but the quiet embodiment of law itself. Through their hands the cosmos held its order; through their silence, life and death found their appointed time.

Clotho, spinner of beginnings, drew the thread of life from the wheel of becoming. From her touch sprang birth, the fragile shimmer of existence taking form from the void. Lachesis, the measurer, received that thread and marked its course with calm precision, setting the rhythm of days, the span of years, the unseen intersections of love, loss, and destiny. And Atropos, the eldest and most solemn, stood apart in stillness, her shears gleaming in the shadow of endings. When the moment arrived, she cut the thread clean, releasing each soul into silence.

No altar rose in their honor, no hymn dared name them. Yet the Greeks revered them above all, for even Zeus bent to their design. Theirs was the power that held heaven and earth in balance, the boundary that not even immortals could cross. They wove the destiny of heroes and beggars alike, the fate of kingdoms and the fall of kings, each strand shining for a time before vanishing into the tapestry of eternity.

To behold the Moirai was to glimpse the architecture of the divine that every birth carried its ending, and every ending, its place within the greater weave. They did not punish, only preserved. Without their measured hands, the cosmos would unravel, and the harmony that bound mortal and immortal alike would be lost to chaos.

Bound by the Thread

To the ancient Greeks, fate was not a proclamation shouted by the gods, but a quiet current beneath all existence, a sacred law that flowed unseen through heaven and earth alike. The Moirai did not impose destiny. They revealed it. Each thread they spun was drawn from the same loom that bound the stars, the seasons, and the souls of humankind. Through their art, the Greeks discerned that life itself was not chaos, but design, an order measured by hallowed necessity.

The thread of fate, once set in motion, allowed no escape, yet within its tension lived the question of how one would meet it. The coward and the hero might share the same span of years, but their choices gave that thread its color. In this, the Greeks found dignity amid inevitability. Fate defined the limits of life, but character defined its meaning.

Heroes such as Achilles embodied that paradox. Offered the choice between a quiet life and a brief blaze of glory, he accepted the path of remembrance, knowing his end was already sealed. Fate could not be defied, but it could be fulfilled with courage. This truth lay at the heart of every tragedy. The gods decree the end, but mortals determine the manner of their fall.

Even Zeus, lord of the storm, bowed before this order. When Sarpedon's death drew near, the father of gods ached to intervene, but to unweave the thread was to unmake the world. So the Moirai remained supreme, silent arbiters of necessity, and through their art the Greeks saw that mortality itself was sacred, not because it endured, but because it must end.

Threads That Cross the Veil

Though the Moirai did not reign within the Underworld, their dominion over destiny bound them in spirit to its depths. Every soul that crossed the veil into Hades' realm had first passed beneath the shears of Atropos, whose hand severed the thread of life when its span was complete. The judges of the dead—Minos, Rhadamanthys, and Aeacus—pronounced their verdicts, but those judgments merely honored the design long woven by the Fates.

In certain myths, the Moirai stood sentinel at the shadowed threshold of the afterlife, observing the silent passage of souls. Their presence at the gates symbolized more than mere transition. It affirmed the divine architecture of destiny. Even the River Styx, that sacred boundary between the worlds of breath and silence, bore their imprint. As Clotho spun the thread of life above, so Charon ferried souls below, completing the journey charted by their decree.

Yet not all bowed to their eternal order. The Orphic Mysteries whispered of a path beyond fate, a cycle that could be broken through purification, remembrance, and divine ascent. In Orphic belief, the soul could transcend the wheel of rebirth, escaping the bonds the Moirai had spun. It was a radical vision, one that reimagined destiny as a veil that could be lifted, rather than a wall that must be obeyed.

Still, the vast tapestry of Greek mythology upheld the supremacy of the Moirai. Whether beneath the earth or beneath the stars, their presence was unshakable. Through every soul and every silence, they reminded all, mortal and immortal, that fate, once spun, must always be fulfilled.

Spinners of the Final Truth

The Moirai stood at the axis of all creation, neither cruel nor kind, but absolute. Through their hands passed the birth and death of every soul, mortal or otherwise. They did not command the storm nor calm the sea. They simply wove the pattern that made both possible. Their silence was the voice of order, their stillness the pulse of eternity.

Clotho's spindle turned at the first cry of life. Lachesis measured the span unseen, marking each joy and sorrow along the thread. And when Atropos raised her shears, even the gods held their breath, for her cut did not end the story, it completed it. In that moment, the Greeks saw not punishment but perfection, that the design of existence lay not in its length, but in its purpose.

So the Fates endured, inviolate and eternal, the unseen hands that bind heaven and earth. They remind us that destiny is not an enemy to resist, but a law to understand; not the end of freedom, but its frame. For within the thread they spin lies the mystery of all things. Every life, no matter how brief, is part of a greater weave that never unravels.

FORETOLD IN SHADOW

In the mythic vision of ancient Greece, prophecy was not mere foresight, but fate unveiled before its time—unyielding, cryptic, and often unheeded. It was both revelation and curse, a celestial echo of the thread already spun. Even the gods bowed to its command, for prophecy did not alter destiny. It confirmed it. Nowhere did its shadow fall more deeply than upon the Underworld, where souls carried the weight of what had long been foretold. The living sought the oracles for glimpses beyond the mortal shroud, while the dead lingered in tales of those who tried—and failed—to flee their doom. In every myth, prophecy stood not as warning, but as mirror, reflecting the inescapable pattern of what must come to pass.

> *"No man may escape the doom spun by the Fates,*
> *Nor outrun the words of the seers,*
> *For what is foretold in shadow shall rise in light."*
> — Pindar, *Pythian Odes*

Seers of Shadow and Flame

Oracles were the living conduits of divine will, mortal voices through which the gods revealed what lay beyond mortal knowing. The most radiant among them was the Pythia of Delphi, priestess of Apollo, who inhaled sacred vapors and spoke in riddles shaped by the god of prophecy. Though her shrine was crowned in light, her words often pierced the darkness, touching upon death, destiny, and the mysteries of Hades' domain.

Yet it was at the Necromanteion, the Oracle of the Dead, that mortals sought prophecy from the afterlife itself. Standing near the dark waters of the Acheron, this temple was revered as a threshold between worlds. Pilgrims came with offerings and ritual intent, summoning voices unbound by time. They believed the dead, released from the blindness of life, could see what the living could not, that beyond the silence of death lay knowledge unshaded by illusion.

In Homer's *Odyssey*, Odysseus descends to consult the prophet Tiresias, who, though dead, beholds truth with unclouded sight. From him Odysseus learns that foreknowledge is not freedom, for even the wise cannot unmake what the Fates have decreed. The blind prophet sees all paths, yet none lead beyond destiny. Through such tales, the Greeks perceived prophecy not as escape, but as illumination, an acknowledgment that to know one's fate is not to avoid it, but to face it with understanding.

The Prophetic Bridge

Prophecy, in its truest form, was less prediction than preparation, a sacred alignment of the soul with what eternity required. Through the voice of seers, the visions of priestesses, and the whispers of the dead, mortals were granted the grace not of avoidance, but of awareness. In this light, prophecy became a bridge between the living and the dead, the present and the eternal, guiding all toward their ordained end with dignity and comprehension.

Plato's *Myth of Er* offered a vision of this cosmic rhythm. The fallen warrior, returned from death, bore witness to the judgment of souls and the choosing of new lives, a revelation that providence was not linear but cyclical, ever renewing through memory and choice. In his words, prophecy became philosophy, the remembrance of divine order made manifest.

In Virgil's *Aeneid*, prophecy descends again into the abyss below, where Aeneas meets the spirit of his father Anchises. There, the future of Rome is unveiled—not as possibility, but as inevitability—and from that revelation the living world is set in motion. Even the afterlife became an architect of destiny, its shadows shaping empires yet unborn.

Among ordinary mortals, prophecy was woven into daily life. Before voyage or war, before marriage or mourning, offerings were made to hear the will of the gods. In funeral rites, prophecy's echo lingered, each chant and libation meant not merely to honor the dead, but to align the soul with its destined passage. Thus, even in silence, prophecy endured, the luminous thread that stitched together life, death, and the eternal return.

To Defy Fate

Though fate was deemed unbreakable, Greek myth is filled with those who dared its thread. Mortals and demigods alike struggled against the design woven by the Moirai. Some fled from prophecy, others ignored divine warning, and a few sought to outwit death itself. Yet in every defiance, destiny prevailed, often in ways crueler than imagined. These tales do not mock human will. They honor it, even as they reveal its limits. For in resisting what was foretold, mortals illuminated a sacred truth. Fate may be challenged or delayed, but never undone.

> *"No man may escape his fate, not even the gods themselves."*
> — Homer, *The Iliad*

Blind March of Destiny

Among all who wrestled with prophecy, none walked its crueler path than Oedipus. Before his first cry, the oracle had spoken. He would slay his father and wed his mother. In terror, his parents cast him out to die upon the mountainside. Yet fate is not undone by brutality. Rescued and raised in ignorance, he fled what he believed his doom, only to meet it in disguise.

On a lonely road, he quarreled with a stranger and struck him dead—his true father, King Laius. Later, he solved the riddle of the Sphinx, gained the throne of Thebes, and married Queen Jocasta, his mother. In fleeing fate, he fulfilled it. The prophecy had not pursued him. It had waited, certain of its hour.

Mortal Thread

Achilles, born of the sea-nymph Thetis and a mortal king, was fated for greatness, and an early death. To guard him, his mother plunged him into the River Styx, leaving only the heel by which she held him untouched. When told he must choose between long life or immortal glory through a brief one, he chose the flame over the embers.

On the plains of Troy, his wrath reshaped the war, yet even he could not outrun his measure. Guided by Apollo, Paris loosed an arrow that found the only mortal part of his flesh. Achilles fell, not in defeat, but in fulfillment. His legend endures because he met fate not with fear, but with acceptance, proving that even doom can burn with purpose.

Ascent and Fall

Icarus, son of Daedalus, knew no prophecy, only warning. Fleeing the prison of Crete on wings of wax and feather, he was told, "Fly not too low, lest the sea weigh you down, nor too high, lest the sun melt your path." But the thrill of flight consumed him. He rose higher, intoxicated by freedom, until the sun unmade what craft had wrought.

Feathers scattered, the sky released him. He plunged into the sea, vanishing beneath the waves that now bear his name. Icarus's fall was not the wrath of gods but the cost of wonder, reminding humankind that even the sky has laws.

Price of Defiance

Among mortals, none defied the order more cunningly than Sisyphus. With silver tongue and boundless arrogance, he deceived Thanatos, chaining Death itself and halting the passage of souls. For a moment, no one died, and the balance of the world faltered.

But fate is patient. When the order was restored, Sisyphus was condemned to endless labor, pushing a boulder uphill only to see it fall again. His torment mirrored his defiance. Motion without progress, a labor without end. In Hades, he became the emblem of futility, proving that cleverness may delay death, but cannot unmake it.

Reins of Ruin

Phaethon, son of Apollo, burned to prove his divine blood. Against his father's pleas, he seized the reins of the sun-chariot and drove across the sky. The steeds, unbound by mortal command, veered from their path. The heavens flared. Rivers boiled. Earth scorched beneath the wildfire of his ambition.

To save creation, Zeus cast a thunderbolt. The chariot shattered, and Phaethon fell, a comet undone by his own radiance. His death was not vengeance, but consequence. In seeking to wield celestial light, he became its victim, and the world bore his scars.

Unyielding Grip of Fate

The myths of defiance reveal not the viciousness of fate, but its constancy. From oracles and heroes to fools and kings, every struggle returns to the same truth. What is woven must one day be fulfilled. To the Greeks, destiny was not an enemy to be conquered, but a mystery to be understood. In their stories, even rebellion became devotion, for to stand against the inevitable was itself an act of reverence—proof that humanity, though bound, still dares to reach for the divine.

FINAL DECREE

In the mythic vision of the Greeks, death was not an end to be feared, but a sacred threshold, woven into the design of fate and upheld by divine law. No hero, however valiant, nor king, however wise, could sever the thread once it had been spun. The Moirai governed its course, and even the gods bowed to their decree. In these ancient tales, death is neither punishment nor reward but certainty—inevitable, impartial, and eternal. To live was to walk a path already measured; to die was to reach its destined end.

> *"No mortal man, nor even the mightiest of kings,*
> *Can flee the shadowy grasp of death,*
> *For the fate spun at birth shall always find its end."*
> — Homer, *Iliad*

Fate Above All

The ancient Greeks believed that fate, or moira, was a fundamental law of existence, inescapable and absolute. Unlike other spiritual forces, it could not be influenced by prayer, bribed with sacrifice, or undone by heroism. Fate was not a form of punishment or reward. It was the framework upon which all life was structured, a sacred pattern spun by the Moirai and respected by mortals and gods alike.

Clotho, Lachesis, and Atropos determined every soul's course from birth to death. Those who sought to escape their fate, only hastened it. Achilles stands as the exemplar, choosing flame over shadow, death over obscurity. His choice embodied kleos, the immortal glory that transcends the grave. In ancient Greece, fate was not a ill-spirited force, but a comic order that gave meaning to existence. The wise accepted their lot with courage, while the proud who tried to resist it often fell. Fate was not an enemy, but the harmony that held the universe together.

Instruments of Destiny

In Greek mythology, the moira reigned supreme, even over the gods themselves. Yet while they could not rewrite destiny's final decree, the gods often shaped how it unfolded. They served as agents of destiny rather than its architects, influencing the paths mortals took to arrive at their final ends.

The Olympians were deeply entwined with mortal affairs. Some extended favor, offering aid and insight, while others unleashed wrath, intensifying suffering. Apollo, god of prophecy, revealed fate's outline through his oracle at Delphi. His cryptic messages did not prevent what was to happen. The messages ensured it, nudging mortals toward choices that fulfilled destiny's design.

Athena acted as a strategist, aiding heroes like Odysseus with wisdom and guidance. She could not alter his fate, but she refined the course he sailed. Conversely, Poseidon, angered by Odysseus, prolonged his suffering without derailing his return. Similarly, Hera's persecution of Heracles caused endless trials, yet could not deny him apotheosis.

Oedipus's tragedy reveals this balance most clearly. Warned by Apollo's oracle that he would kill his father and wed his mother, he fled, only to fulfill the prophecy by flight itself. The gods did not craft his ruin. They ensured its order. In every tale, the Olympians act as stewards of inevitability, shaping mortal struggle while leaving destiny untouched.

Death, Destiny, and the Soul

Greek philosophy sought to probe the very foundations of fate and mortality. While mythology presented fate as an inexorable force through story and symbol, the philosophers of Classical Greece aimed to interpret its implications for the soul, ethics, and the pursuit of wisdom.

Plato, in *The Republic*, envisioned death as transformation rather than annihilation. In the *Myth of Er*, he described souls judged and set upon new paths, affirming that moral choice echoes beyond the grave. Fate, for Plato, was not blind. It was justice woven through eternity.

Aristotle, though less metaphysical, viewed fate as a structural force rather than a fixed decree. While he acknowledged life's limitations, he emphasized virtue and reasoned action. For Aristotle, human flourishing, or eudaimonia, came from making moral choices within one's natural purpose. Destiny might set the stage, but character determined the performance.

The Stoics took a starker view. Thinkers like Epictetus and Marcus Aurelius saw fate as an unyielding cosmic order, an intelligent force aligning all events. To resist it was to suffer, to embrace it was to live wisely. Stoicism taught acceptance not as surrender, but as liberation, a harmony between the individual and the universe.

Whether in myth or philosophy, Greek thought always returned to a central truth. Death is not to be feared, and fate is not to be fought. It is in how one meets the inevitable—with virtue, clarity, and courage—that meaning is found. In the face of mortality, the Greeks did not seek escape, but understanding.

LAST THREAD CUT

Greek mythology and philosophy converge upon a single, unyielding truth. Fate is inescapable. Whether spun by the Moirai or foreseen by the oracles, destiny ruled gods and mortals alike. Prophecy offered only glimpses of what must come, yet every attempt to flee its design only hastened fulfillment. From Achilles' pursuit of glory over life to Oedipus' desperate flight from his doom, the myths reveal a universe where fate could not be bargained with, only met.

Yet this struggle with destiny was not Greece's alone. Across the ancient world, civilizations wrestled with the same eternal questions. Is the path of life prewritten, or can the soul alter its course? Can death be delayed, or merely understood? In the pages ahead, we journey beyond Hellenic shores, to the lands of Egypt, Mesopotamia, and the North, to explore how other cultures conceived their own reckonings with time, prophecy, and the end of all things. Each civilization wove its answer into the same immortal tapestry, the human search for meaning in the shadow of fate.

CHAPTER 11

TWO VISIONS

HADES · PLVTO

Eternal Realms

The ancient Greeks and Romans gazed upon death as one might gaze into still water, seeing shadow, not nothingness. In that reflection, they envisioned an Underworld vast, eternal, and ruled by fate. Here, every soul crossed the veil for divine judgment, before the chthonic powers who upheld the laws of the dead. Yet while the Romans drew deeply from Greek tradition, they did not merely inherit. They reshaped. Hades became Pluto; myth was recast in the language of empire. Through this transformation, the Underworld became more than a realm of the departed. It became a mirror of the living, reflecting each culture's fears, hopes, and yearning to know what lies beyond the mortal veil.

> *"There is a place in the Underworld, vast and shadowed,*
> *Where souls of the dead must pass,*
> *Through judgment's gate, to their fated rest."*
> — Virgil, *Aeneid*

Evolution of the Shadow Gods

Though Hades and Pluto are often spoken of as one, their natures reveal the souls of two civilizations. In Greece, Hades reigned in solemn silence—remote, unyielding, and feared not for malice, but for inevitability. He punished none, yet few dared utter his name, lest misfortune follow. Within his dark halls beside Persephone, he kept the balance of the living and the dead, a warden of the boundary who asked for no worship and offered no favor.

Rome reshaped this still shadow into radiance. The name Plouton, or giver of wealth, was not shunned but invoked, a patron of fertility and hidden treasure. To Roman eyes, the depths of the earth were not solely graves, but vaults of abundance with gold, silver, and the fruiting soil that sustained the world. In Pluto's dominion, death and renewal became twin forces, the harvest and the grave bound by one divine law.

Where Hades ruled in hush, Pluto was praised in hymns. The dread of death softened into reverence. The god once cloaked in fear was honored as a source of prosperity and return. Yet beneath both masks abides the same truth. Whether called Hades or Pluto, the ruler of the dead stands eternal—guardian of passage, keeper of silence, steward of the soul's last crossing.

Afterlife Reforged

The Romans drew deeply from Greek tradition, not as imitators but as refashioners. In Virgil's *Aeneid*, the descent of Aeneas mirrors that of Odysseus in the *Odyssey*, yet the worlds they enter could not be more different.

Odysseus calls the dead from shadow, while Aeneas walks amongst them. In Homer's realm, the abyss below is a twilight of echoes, where shades wander joyless and forgotten. But Virgil's landscape is deliberate, a hierarchy of justice where every soul meets the weight of its deeds. The wicked descend to torment, the virtuous ascend to Elysium, and all are judged by eternal measure.

Here, too, a new mystery arises. Those who drink from Lethe return to life, their memories veiled. Greek philosophy had dreamed of such rebirth, and Rome made it law. The Stoic and the Pythagorean alike found in Virgil's verses a vision of the soul's renewal, a moral order extending beyond death.

In Rome's hands, the chthonic domain became a mirror of its own empire; structured, moral, inexorable. Where Greece saw death as silence, Rome saw it as sentence, a reckoning through which legacy endures. Yet across centuries of conquest and creed, the old stories endured, carried from Greece to Rome like sacred flame passed from hand to hand.

Shared Myths

Though the ancient Greek and Roman civilizations shaped the afterlife through different eyes, their deepest myths endured, passed like sacred fire from one world to the next. These tales crossed centuries unbroken, their forms shifting, their meaning unchanged. They spoke of love and loss, of judgment and justice, and of the fragile bridge between life and eternity.

Foremost among them was the sorrow of Orpheus and Eurydice, the mortal musician whose song reached even the heart of death. Both nations sang of his descent and his undoing, a tale reminding mortals that love may move the gods but not overturn the laws of fate. The three judges of the dead also stood eternal, presiding over the souls of mortals in both Greek and Roman belief, their verdicts echoing the moral balance each civilization held dear.

The punishments of Sisyphus and Tantalus likewise endured, symbols of arrogance chained to futility, lessons carved in the bedrock of the abyss below. Their endless labors spoke not of divine cruelty, but of order restored, each sin answered by its mirror.

Yet no myth bridged the two worlds more completely than that of Persephone, called Proserpina by Rome. Her descent and return gave rhythm to the seasons and meaning to mortality itself. Through her, both Greece and Rome glimpsed the same eternal truth that death is not erasure but renewal, and that the cycle of loss and return binds the living to the gods.

Twilight of Two Empires

The Underworlds of Greece and Rome were bound by shared myths and mirrored deities, yet each bore the distinct imprint of its civilization's soul. Hades and Pluto, though brothers in form, reflected differing visions, one a silent warden of the dead, the other a god entwined with wealth, legacy, and the hidden veins of the earth. In the *Odyssey*, the afterlife stood as a dim reflection of life, hollow and formless. But in the *Aeneid*, it rose into a dominion of judgment, destiny, and renewal, where souls were measured and reborn.

Myths like Orpheus and Eurydice, the three judges, and the punishments of Tartarus endured, but as they crossed the threshold into Roman thought, they took on new weight, shaped by duty, consequence, and empire.

Together, they forged a legacy that outlasted marble and empire alike, a vision of the afterlife not as oblivion, but as sacred passage, where the divine and mortal meet once more beneath the shadow of eternity.

ACROSS THE ANCIENT WORLD

A shadowed realm beyond death is not unique to Greece, for across the ancient world, cultures gazed into the same eternal abyss and shaped it with their own truths. From the deserts of Egypt to the icy reaches of the North, mythmakers gave voice to the providence that awaits all mortals. In Duat, the Egyptians envisioned a perilous journey of the soul, where truth outweighed kingship itself. The Norse spoke of Hel, a cold and silent world beneath the roots of Yggdrasil, where those who died without valor were gathered. In Mesopotamia, the Underworld was a house of dust, where all were stripped of name and glory. Though these realms differed in form and godhood, their echoes ring alike, each speaks of judgment, of separation, and of a fate no soul may outrun. Through these stories, the Underworld becomes a mirror held to the mystery of death itself.

> "Beneath the earth there lies a realm unseen,
> A shadowed land where all must go,
> Bound by fate to dwell beyond the light."
> — Homer, *Odyssey*

Weight of a Heart

In the sacred imagination of Egypt, the Duat stretched beneath the living world, a labyrinth of shadow and flame, vast and perilous, yet sanctified beneath the eternal gaze of Osiris, lord of the dead. While Greece envisioned stillness and shadow, the Duat shimmered with paradox, a place of dread and passage, terror and transcendence. At death, the soul began its pilgrimage through this hidden realm, threading past serpent-headed sentinels and guardians wrought of fire and fang—demons born of shadow. Each gate was a trial, each terror a mirror—testing not the body, but the truth of the spirit, until at last the soul stood in the hall of final judgment.

There, at the heart of eternity, unfolded the most solemn rite, the weighing of the heart. Before Osiris and his tribunal, the heart of the departed was laid upon the golden scales and measured against the feather of Ma'at—the goddess of truth, justice, and cosmic order. If the heart rose light—unburdened by falsehood or cruelty, the soul passed into the Field of Reeds, where sunlit waters never stilled and harvests never failed, a perfected vision of life, eternal and serene. But if the heart sank heavy with sin, it was hurled into the maw of Ammit, the Devourer, whose form bore the crocodile, lion, and hippopotamus—the fiercest of beasts. To be consumed by her was no torment but oblivion itself. The soul undone, struck from memory and from the wheel of rebirth.

Where the Greeks spoke of judgement and inevitability, the Egyptians proclaimed trial and truth. Their afterlife was no descent into shadow, but a crucible of spirit, where every deed was weighed and destiny forged anew. In the Duat, eternity was not granted by fate, but earned by the integrity of one's heart.

Where No Valkyries Ride

Beneath the roots of Yggdrasil, the World Tree, lay the realm of Hel, a land of frost and shadow, where silence clung like mist and no sunbeam ever strayed. This kingdom belonged to Hel, daughter of Loki, whose half-living visage mirrored the threshold she ruled. Unlike the burning infernos imagined in later Christian visions, the Norse Underworld was a realm of cold stillness, where the sick, the aged, and those who died without honor found their final rest. Only warriors who perished in glory were borne aloft by Odin's Valkyries to feast in Valhalla. All others descended into Hel's embrace, where memory lingered heavy in the air and the living world grew faint as a dream.

Like the shadowed meadows of Greek lore, most souls in Hel drifted in pallid suspension, neither exalted nor tormented, but bound to an existence stripped of joy and longing. Yet the world held darker places. In the bitter reaches of Náströnd, the Shore of Corpses, oath-breakers, murderers, and traitors were condemned. There, under a sky dripping venom and frozen night, the serpent Níðhöggr coiled and fed, gnawing eternally upon the bodies of the damned. Their fate mirrored that of Tartarus, where Greek transgressors endured punishments sculpted from their crimes.

Yet Hel herself was no tormentor. Like Hades, she reigned with solemn detachment, an impartial warden of boundaries. She passed no verdicts, but held her kingdom in austere stillness, ensuring that no soul might wander back into the world of the living. Stern, inevitable, enduring—Hel embodied the ancient law of balance, the quiet keeper of death's domain, as necessary as the roots that bind the worlds of gods and mortals.

Descent Through Seven Gates

In the myths of ancient Mesopotamia, the dead descended to the Land of No Return—a realm of dust and silence, ruled by the stern goddess Ereshkigal. Here, unlike in Greece where souls were judged and divided, all shared the same bleak destiny. Kings and beggars, warriors and shepherds—every life, no matter how great, was leveled by death, each soul clothed in shadow and fed on dust.

The most haunting tale of this dominion is the Descent of Inanna. The goddess of love and war sought her sister Ereshkigal, but to pass the seven gates of the Underworld she surrendered crown, jewels, and raiment—each token of power stripped away until she stood naked before the Queen of Shadows. There she was judged, struck down, and hung upon a hook—her glory extinguished in silence. Only through divine intervention was she restored, yet her release demanded a price. Her consort Dumuzi was taken in her stead, bound to the Underworld for half the year—his absence marking the earth's barren season until his return restored the world to life.

Like Persephone's descent, Inanna's ordeal revealed the sacred rhythm of decay and renewal. Yet the Mesopotamian Underworld remained more final, more absolute—a realm of sealed gates and inexorable law, where escape was rare and even gods paid the cost of mortality.

The Shining Otherworld

In the Celtic imagination, death opened not upon darkness but upon Annwn, a shimmering Otherworld of beauty and abundance. Green hills rolled beneath ever-bright sunlight; feasts never ended, and music drifted on enchanted air. Presiding over this realm was Arawn, a shadowed yet noble king who governed the souls of the dead. Unlike Hades, bound forever to his dark dominion, Arawn could cross into the mortal world—even trading places with men. In the Welsh tale of Pwyll, a mortal prince ruled Annwn in Arawn's stead—proving that, for a time, the boundary between worlds could be crossed.

Yet Annwn was not without peril or test. In later tales it held within it Caer Sidi—a fortress veiled in mist, where enchantments and trials awaited the dead. Those who passed its tests might taste paradise; others were ensnared in its riddles. In this way, the Celtic vision resembled the Elysium of Greece, where the most noble souls found blessed repose, and yet it also echoed the shadowed trials of Hades' domain.

To the Celts, the afterlife was not a descent into silence, but a passage into mystery—a realm both wondrous and perilous, where kings ruled in twilight and the soul's journey flowed beyond the grave.

Fires of Naraka

In the vast cosmology of Hindu belief, the Underworld is called Naraka—a realm of shadowed passage where the soul descends to reckon with the weight of its deeds. Unlike the eternal prisons of Tartarus, Naraka was not a place without end, but a crucible of purification. Here, beneath the gaze of Yama, the god of death and stern judge of souls—each spirit faced the consequences of its deeds, walking through trials wrought by the law of karma.

Naraka was divided into many realms, each a mirror of sin and recompense. The deceitful, the violent, the cruel—all endured torments shaped by the wrongs they wrought in life. Yet these punishments, however dreadful, were never eternal. They were the fires of cleansing, purging the soul of its burden so that it may rise again. When the debt was repaid, the spirit was freed from Naraka's grasp—reborn into the wheel of life, its path shaped anew by the echoes of what had been.

In this vision, death was not a closed gate, but a turning. Where the Greeks imagined fate as fixed, the Hindus saw the soul as a wanderer, moving through cycles of death and rebirth, ever seeking release. Through Naraka, even the darkest stain could be burned away—for truth and renewal lay at the heart of existence. In this faith, the Underworld was not an end, but a forge—where from suffering, the soul might rise transformed toward its higher destiny.

Where All Souls Journey

Across the ancient world, myths of the Underworld offer a mirror to the soul's final mystery, a question whispered in every land. What lies beyond the veil? Though each culture shaped its vision through the lens of its own faith, all sought to illuminate the unseen path. The Egyptians envisioned the afterlife as a tribunal of truth, where each heart was weighed against cosmic order. The Norse saw death as a thread in fate's vast tapestry, woven with honor and valor. In Mesopotamia, the Land of No Return stood in silence—grim, inevitable, and absolute. The Celts, by contrast, dreamt of Annwn, a realm of beauty laced with riddles, where the soul wandered through shadow and splendor. And in the sacred fires of Naraka, the Hindus found not finality but purification—suffering as the gate through which the soul must pass to be reborn. Though these visions differ in form, they share a deeper truth, that in every land and tongue, the question of the afterlife stirs the human spirit—to imagine, to fear, and to hope for what lies beyond the veil.

ECHOES OF THE UNDERWORLD

Though millennia have passed, the myths of the Underworld still cast their shadows across the human imagination. Their visions—of judgment and renewal, of reward and punishment—have seeped into the foundations of modern belief. From the paradises of Elysium to the torments of Tartarus, these mythic realms continue to echo through the world's religions, philosophies, and stories. Heaven and hell, purgatory and paradise—all bear the imprint of older worlds, where gods weighed souls and gates divided the living from the dead. Even today, in sacred texts, speculative fiction, and whispered prayers, we revisit those archetypal paths; the righteous ascending, the wicked descending, the soul moving through mystery toward meaning. The Underworld exists—not as relic, but as mirror to our hopes, our fears, and our longing for what lies beyond. It is reborn in every age—reshaped but never forgotten.

> *"The soul of man is immortal and imperishable,*
> *passing through many realms,*
> *until it reaches the place where truth and justice reign."*
> — Plato, *Phaedrus*

Eternal Court

Among the most enduring legacies of Greek mythology is the vision of death not as end, but as passage—where the soul is summoned to judgment and appointed its eternal place. This belief, echoing across civilizations, reveals a truth deeply rooted in human thought that the deeds of life shape the destiny of the dead. The idea that morality binds the soul beyond death reappears across ages, each tradition casting judgment as the threshold between shadow and eternity.

In ancient Greece, this role fell to Minos, Rhadamanthus, and Aeacus, who weighed the lives of mortals and decreed their fates. The virtuous entered Elysium, a realm of light and harmony. The ordinary dwelled in the Asphodel Meadows, living in muted shadow. The evil and wicked were condemned to Tartarus, where their crimes found eternal reflection in torment. This division foreshadowed the later visions of heaven, purgatory, and hell, where souls are likewise sorted by worth.

So too did Egypt weave morality into its vision of death. There, the dead stood before Osiris, their hearts weighed against the feather of Ma'at, goddess of truth. A heart proven light entered the Field of Reeds, a paradise of renewal. But one heavy with sin was devoured by Ammit, a fate darker than torment—annihilation. Like the Greek Underworld, the Egyptian afterlife mirrored the scales of justice, binding eternity to the choices of mortal life.

These echoes resound in later faiths. In Christianity, the Last Judgment separates souls to heaven or hell, while in Islam, the righteous cross safely over the bridge spanning hell, and the unworthy fall into its fire. Even in secular tales, literature and film alike, death is imagined as a reckoning, an inescapable moment when one's life is measured. That this theme endures across time and culture reveals its power. Humanity has always believed that death is not silence, but consequence.

A Soul's Path Across Myth

Greek myth cast a long shadow over Western thought, shaping how generations imagined death, judgment, and the fate of the soul. As Hellenistic culture spread and mingled with Roman tradition, its visions of the Underworld became entwined with other faiths and philosophies, leaving an enduring imprint on how later civilizations imagined what lies beyond the grave.

In early Christianity, echoes of Greek and Roman belief resound unmistakably. The division of the blessed in Elysium and the damned in Tartarus foreshadows the Christian pairing of heaven and hell. The fiery abyss of eternal torment, so vividly portrayed in Dante's *Inferno*, descends in part from Greek images of Tartarus and Roman visions of the realm of Dis Pater—though the latter, in his earliest form, was not a punisher but a sovereign of the dead.

The influence of Hellenic thought also reached into Jewish eschatology. The shadowed realm of Sheol, once a neutral resting place of the dead, gradually transformed into a domain where moral judgment and separation took hold. This evolution reflects the current of Hellenistic philosophy, which pressed upon Hebrew tradition the idea that death was not the same for all, but carried consequence.

Greek philosophy carried forward those visions of the afterlife. In Plato's *Myth of Er*, found in *The Republic*, the soul journeys through judgment, choosing new lives and passing through cycles of rebirth. This vision shaped not only later Neoplatonism, but also threads of early Christian mysticism, where reincarnation, purification, and ascent of the soul were debated with urgency and awe. Even modern spiritual movements, such as New Age thought, inherit this ancient legacy—echoing Orphic rites and Pythagorean teachings when speaking of karma, soul-evolution, and the passage toward higher realms.

Beyond the halls of philosophy and theology, Greek myth also shaped rites of death itself. The ancient practice of placing a coin with the deceased to pay Charon, the ferryman of souls, endures in echoes across cultures. Today, families still place tokens or objects with the dead, offerings meant to aid safe passage through the mysteries that follow life. Such customs reveal how enduring the Greek vision remains—that the journey into shadow is perilous, and that the living must prepare the soul for its crossing.

Ancient Gates in Modern Worlds

Beyond the spheres of religion and philosophy, the Greek Underworld left an indelible mark upon modern fantasy, shaping the landscapes of literature, film, and popular imagination. The vision of a shadowed land of the dead, governed by divine order and traversed by heroes, remains one of humanity's most powerful storytelling devices.

Many of the great architects of modern fantasy drew directly from these ancient roots. In J.R.R. Tolkien's Middle-earth, the Halls of Mandos, where souls await their fate, echo the solemn chambers of Hades. In C.S. Lewis' *Chronicles of Narnia*, the themes of sacrifice, death, and return are woven with threads reminiscent of the Orphic Mysteries and the rebirth of Persephone. These echoes reveal that even in modern mythmaking, the Greek vision of death remains a compass for the imagination.

Video games, films, and television series have likewise descended into these ancient shadows. Titles such as Hades, God of War, and Final Fantasy pit mortals against gods of the dead or confront them with labyrinthine domains of judgment and escape. In series like *Supernatural, Percy Jackson & the Olympians*, and *American Gods*, the myths of Tartarus, Elysium, and the ferryman's crossing are reborn in new guises, reminding audiences that the gates of the Underworld are never far from modern tales.

The archetype of the hero's descent—katabasis—remains among the most enduring motifs in world literature. From Orpheus, Heracles, and Odysseus, who braved Hades, to Dante, who journeyed through the infernal circles, to Harry Potter, who passes into death and returns transformed, the pattern persists. Each tale affirms that to face the Underworld is to confront the deepest truths of the self and to emerge forever changed.

Nor is this influence confined to the West. In Japanese anime and manga—such as Yu Yu Hakusho, Naruto, and Bleach—heroes descend into realms strikingly similar to Greek and Roman afterlives, structured with guardians, hierarchies, and places of trial. Across cultures and genres, the same vision endures that the journey through death is not simply an end, but the most profound of passages, where fate, justice, and transformation await.

Shadows Beyond Time

The myths of the Greek Underworld left an enduring imprint upon how humanity conceives of death, judgment, and the soul's fate. Themes of moral reckoning, divine justice, and the passage of the spirit shaped religions, philosophies, and cultural traditions across centuries. From echoes of Elysium and Tartarus in later visions of heaven and hell, to their reappearance in art and story, these Greek foundations continue to shape how we imagine the afterlife. So long as humanity contemplates the mystery beyond death, the myths of Hades and his shadowed realm shall remain alive—in thought, in story, in the eternal mirror of the soul.

BEYOND THE VEIL OF MEMORY

The echoes of the Underworld do not fade. They transform. Across centuries, the myths of Hades and Pluto, of Osiris, Hel, and Naraka, have passed like sacred embers from one age to the next. Each retelling rekindles the same eternal question. What becomes of the soul when breath departs?

In temples and scriptures, in poetry and art, the afterlife was shaped anew, yet always by the same invisible hand. The Greeks imagined judgment beneath the earth; the Egyptians weighed hearts against truth; the Hindus saw purification in flame. And still, in the quiet of modern thought, those ancient fires burn.

The Underworld endures, not beneath us, but within us. It lives wherever we confront loss and meaning, wherever we ask what lies beyond the gate of life. In that question, myth becomes memory, and memory becomes faith. Thus the journey continues, from shadow to light, from the realms of the dead to the hopes of the living.

We ascend from the Underworld to the realm of prophecy reborn—where sacred words, divine signs, and mortal visions forge the link between gods and humankind. The myths of fate have been spoken; now we turn to the myths of revelation.

CHAPTER 12

BEYOND MYTH

Through the Shadows

From the ancient songs of poets to the silver screens of modern film, Hades and his Underworld have remained inexhaustible sources of wonder and dread. Writers and visionaries have transformed his dominion from mythic origin to a symbol of fate, justice, and the hidden paths of the soul. In Dante's *Inferno*, the abyss deepened into a cathedral of torment and divine order; in modern fantasy, the Underworld reemerges as a shifting landscape of shadow and trial—part terror, part revelation. On film, Hades himself has worn many faces. The stern and distant sovereign of the dead, the usurper who defies Olympus, and at times the solitary god whose silence renders him tragic rather than cruel. Across centuries and across mediums, each retelling reshapes how audiences behold the ruler of shadows and the realm from which no soul returns.

> *"Not even the gods themselves can escape his realm,*
> *For once the gates of Hades close,*
> *No soul may return without his leave."*
> — Homer, *Iliad*

Gates Recast

One of the most profound reimaginings of the Underworld emerged in the early fourteenth century with Dante Alighieri's *Inferno*, the opening canticle of *The Divine Comedy*. Though born of Christian theology, Dante's hell carries the echo of Hades' kingdom, its darkness rooted in older myth.

He envisioned the abyss as nine descending circles, each a chamber of punishment where mortal sin met eternal consequence. This order mirrors Tartarus, the Greek abyss where transgressors endured torments shaped by their crimes. At the threshold he placed Minos, the judge of souls, borrowed from Greek legend and recast as a monstrous arbiter, coiling his serpent's tail to mark the damned.

Yet Dante was not the first to descend into that shadow. Long before him, Virgil's *Aeneid* had guided readers through a Roman vision of the afterlife, where Aeneas beheld his father's shade and the fates of the yet unborn. There too the realms divided—the blessed apart from the condemned—a structure that later faiths would inherit.

Over time, these traditions entwined, fusing Greek and Roman imagery with Christian visions of sin and salvation. Hades himself was remade, not as the impartial keeper of death, but as a figure of torment and despair. Thus, the silent sovereign of antiquity gave way to a darker inheritance, one of fire, fear, and divine retribution.

Myth to Fantasy

The myths of Greece continue to breathe through the pages of modern fantasy. The abyss below is endlessly reimagined—its rivers, gates, and rulers reborn in new voices and visions. Countless authors have drawn upon the architecture of Hades' realm, weaving judges of the dead, shadowed dominions, and hallowed reckonings into the fabric of contemporary storytelling.

Among the most celebrated is Rick Riordan's *Percy Jackson & The Olympians*, where Hades appears not as a faceless villain, but as one of the Olympians—stern, weary, and complex. His kingdom remains vast and true to tradition, filled with the River Styx, Cerberus, and the Fields of Asphodel, yet reshaped for modern readers. In this retelling, he becomes not a monster to be defeated, but a god burdened by his duty.

In the dreamlike worlds of Neil Gaiman, the Underworld transforms into a realm of shadow and revelation. In *The Sandman*, the dead move through landscapes of memory and myth; in *American Gods*, the old deities falter, their names fading like embers in the wind of unbelief.

Even in worlds untouched by Greek myth, the shadow of Hades endures. J.R.R. Tolkien's *The Lord of the Rings* introduces the Halls of Mandos, where souls await their passage onward. Though shaped by Norse vision, this destiny bears the cadence of the Greek Underworld, with its division of the blessed and the condemned. In every retelling, death is not an end but an encounter—the moment when the soul beholds its truth.

This fascination persists across genres, especially in young adult fantasy. Leigh Bardugo's *Ninth House* and Madeline Miller's *Circe* return to the ancient descent—the eternal pattern of loss, trial, and return—reshaping encounters with gods and spirits for a new age. In these retellings, the Underworld remains what it has always been. A mirror of the living, where choices are weighed and the soul's fate revealed.

Olympus to Hollywood

On screen, Hades and the Underworld have worn many faces, sometimes rendered as a solemn deity cloaked in shadow, at other times as a villain, trickster, or reluctant sovereign. Cinema has long borrowed from his dominion, weaving myths both faithful and fantastical, reshaping the ruler of the dead for modern imagination.

Among the most recognizable portrayals is Disney's *Hercules* (1997), where Hades is reimagined as a flame-haired schemer, quick of tongue and driven by ambition to usurp Zeus. Far removed from the mythic god who sought no throne beyond his own, this version recasts the king of the Underworld in the mold of a trickster like Loki—comic, cunning, and chaotic—yet it remains one of the most iconic images of him in popular culture.

A darker vision appears in *Clash of the Titans* (2010) and its sequel *Wrath of the Titans* (2012). Here, the silent one becomes a brooding and vengeful figure, set against Zeus and Poseidon, his role transformed from impartial keeper of the dead to adversary and destroyer. Though the films borrow from ancient stories—hinting at Persephone and the Underworld's power—they heighten Hades' presence into that of an active force of wrath, far beyond his mythic neutrality.

More measured is *Percy Jackson & The Olympians: The Lightning Thief* (2010), adapted from Rick Riordan's novels. This portrayal envisions Hades as a weary, reluctant ruler. His Underworld unfurls in vast shadows, filled with features drawn from myth—Styx, Cerberus, and the Fields of Asphodel—offering a vision closer to the ancient world, even amid creative liberties.

Beyond direct adaptations, films like *Coco* (2017) and *Soul* (2020) echo Greek patterns of the afterlife. Both present realms where souls are judged, guided, or reborn, echoing ideas that trace back to Elysium, Tartarus, and the cycles of reincarnation. Even in horror and supernatural cinema, the shadow of Hades lingers. *Constantine* (2005) and *What Dreams May Come* (1998) envision afterlife realms with rivers of the dead, colossal judges, and landscapes that mirror the ancient Underworld.

Myths Wear New Faces

From the visions of medieval poets to the spectacles of modern cinema, the myths of Hades and the Underworld have never ceased to evolve. Dante's *Inferno* reshaped the Greek realm of the dead into a moralized Christian abyss, while contemporary novels reimagine Hades as both dreaded sovereign and misunderstood god. In fantasy literature, the Underworld endures as a stage of trial and revelation, its echoes heard in the works of Rick Riordan, Neil Gaiman, and J.R.R. Tolkien. On screen, Hades has taken on shifting forms—at times the cunning villain of *Hercules*, at others the weary ruler of *Percy Jackson & The Olympians*. Across centuries and across genres, these retellings reveal a god who refuses oblivion, reshaping his dominion with every age that dares retell his story.

Across these depictions, whether whimsical, fearsome, or reverent, Hades remains unchanged in essence. His realm endures as a mirror of death and destiny, reshaped for every age yet never forgotten. From parchment to screen, from prayer to myth, the shadow of Hades endures. A god reborn each time we speak his name, and a kingdom renewed each time the living imagine the world beyond the veil.

DEPICTION IN MODERN MEDIA

The ancient myths of the Underworld continue to cast their shadow across modern creation—reborn in games, cinema, and the visions of artists. In interactive worlds, players move through realms patterned after Hades' dominion, crossing rivers of the dead, confronting guardians, and choosing paths of fate as though they themselves were shades upon the threshold. Television reimagines mythic figures for new ages—Hades, Persephone, and the judges of the dead walking once more among the living. And in art, from the painted urns of antiquity to the glowing screens of today, the afterlife remains a mirror of humanity's awe before death and eternity. Far from fading, these myths shift form. The gates of Hades stand ever open, inviting each generation to reimagine what lies beyond.

> *"Dark and misty are the halls of Hades,*
> *Where phantoms wander in endless shadow,*
> *Seeking the echoes of the world above."*
> — Homer, *Odyssey*

Descent Into Digital Domains

Across recent years, video games have become one of the most powerful mediums for retelling myth, and few landscapes prove as compelling as the Underworld. Dark, mysterious, and bound to fate, it provides a stage for quests of peril and revelation. Players confront legendary beings, wrestle with morality, and step into the shadowed paths once reserved for heroes of old. Some of the most celebrated games of the modern era have drawn directly from Greek mythology, allowing players to walk the halls of Hades' realm and experience its mysteries firsthand.

Among the most acclaimed is Supergiant Games' *Hades* (2020), a rogue-like odyssey that casts players as Zagreus, the defiant son of Hades, seeking escape from his father's kingdom. The game breathes with mythic fidelity—through the presence of Persephone, Nyx, Thanatos, and others; the perilous landscapes of Tartarus, Asphodel, and Elysium; and the figure of Hades himself, stern yet paternal, far more nuanced than the villain so often imagined. Within this retelling, the god of the dead is not stripped of majesty but reshaped with depth, revealing a ruler whose dominion is bound by care as much as command. If *Hades* revealed the god as ruler and father, *God of War* recast him as adversary and abyss.

The God of War series likewise carves its path through the Underworld. Though centered on Kratos' vengeance, the games lead players through realms of death, none more haunting than the Underworld of *God of War III*. There, the River Styx flows in shadow, the shades of the departed drift in endless gloom, and Hades himself rises as a formidable adversary. This vision leans into the abyssal terrors of Greek imagination, presenting the abyss below not as a place of balance but as a crucible of punishment and struggle.

Other titles embrace the Underworld in more abstract guises. The Persona series and Dark Souls evoke labyrinthine domains of shadow, where wandering spirits and trials of judgment echo Greek and Roman lore. In such games, the land of the dead is not a static myth but a living concept—adaptable, inexhaustible, and ever ready to mirror humanity's fear and fascination with death. By inviting players to explore its halls, battle its guardians, and defy its limits, video games transform myth into an interactive descent. Through play, mortals now walk the paths once sung by poets—the Underworld not merely a story to be told, but a realm to be entered, challenged, and, for some, conquered.

Afterlife on Screen

Greek mythology has found enduring life upon the screen, where the stories of gods, heroes, and the Underworld are retold for new generations. Whether in faithful adaptations or myth-inspired fantasies, the figure of Hades and the shadowed domain he rules continue to shift and evolve, revealing fresh dimensions in the ancient tale.

Perhaps the most familiar portrayal appears in Disney's animated series *Hercules* (1998–1999), which builds upon the fiery, fast-talking version of Hades introduced in the 1997 film. Here, the god becomes a source of comedy and chaos, yet the show widens its scope to reveal more of the Underworld—introducing younger audiences to Charon the ferryman, the Fates, and Cerberus, guardians of the dead. Though stylized and whimsical, it planted the seeds of myth, acquainting many with the eternal landscape of Greek belief.

A darker vision arises in Netflix's *Blood of Zeus* (2020), an animated series that breathes new life into the forgotten corners of Greek lore. While Hades himself remains a shadowed presence, the series reveals the role of the Underworld in shaping both mortal and immortal destinies. Its gods are flawed and fallible, yet deeply bound to human struggles, echoing the spirit of classical myth while layering it with new drama and intensity.

Live-action adaptations also summon Hades to television. The much-anticipated Disney adaptation of *Percy Jackson & The Olympians* promises a modern retelling faithful to Rick Riordan's novels. Unlike renderings that brand Hades as villain, this version leans closer to myth—presenting him as stern and severe, yet not evil, a god defined by balance rather than malice.

Beyond direct adaptations, the themes of the Underworld echo through fantasy and supernatural television. Series such as *Supernatural*, *Lucifer*, and *American Gods* explore realms of judgment, death, and destiny that draw heavily from Greek archetypes. Even when Hades himself does not appear, his dominion lingers in every story that dares to measure the soul. From motion to stillness, the myth crossed from screen to canvas—its shadows finding new life in paint and stone.

Immortalized in Art

Long before cinema or game, the Underworld was etched in art—its visions carved, painted, and imagined anew in every age. In ancient Greece, pottery bore the visions of the Underworld. Charon was shown guiding souls across the river, Orpheus descended to reclaim Eurydice, and Heracles wrestled the three-headed Cerberus from his master's gate. These images, stark and solemn, did more than adorn vessels. They proclaimed belief, reminding all who saw them that the realm of Hades was inescapable and eternal.

During the Renaissance, myth was reborn in brush and marble, fused with Christian visions of judgment. Painters such as Peter Paul Rubens and Michelangelo rendered Hades and Persephone with grandeur and weight, transforming the Underworld into a stage of divine drama. Their works reflected not only reverence for antiquity but also the era's fascination with power, fate, and the sovereigns of death.

In the modern age, artists cast the dark abyss anew. Surrealist canvases, fantasy illustration, and digital concept art reimagined the dominion as vast fortresses of shadow, rivers thick with wandering souls, and radiant meadows reminiscent of Elysium, Tartarus, and the Asphodel Fields. Visionaries such as Victoria Francés and Gerald Brom have breathed haunting beauty into the afterlife, marrying Greek myth with gothic sensibilities.

Even today, in the world of pixels and shifting light, the Underworld remains inexhaustible. Each brushstroke, each rendered scene, proves that the myths of Hades exist—reshaped but never forgotten—offering artists across the ages a mirror for humanity's deepest awe before death and the eternal unknown.

Underworld Without End

The myths of Hades and the Underworld remain unbroken threads in the tapestry of creation—reborn through new voices and new mediums. In *Hades* and *God of War*, players descend into shadow. On screen, *Percy Jackson* and *Blood of Zeus* awaken the old gods for new hearts. From painted urns to digital vistas, the Underworld endures as muse and mirror alike. As art and story evolve, so too does the Lord of the Dead—unchanged in essence, ever reborn in form. Through every telling, he reminds the living of one eternal truth, that death is not disappearance, but transformation.

HADES KINGDOM

For millennia, the dominion of Hades has endured—its shadow lengthening across every age, adapting to the visions of those who speak his name. From the hymns of Greece to the philosophies of Rome, from Dante's pen to modern fantasy, the fascination with death, judgment, and fate has never waned. The twilight dominion of Hades remains a mirror for humanity's awe before the unknown, its gates opening anew in each retelling—through literature, art, and the vast expanse of modern media. Each generation redefines him—now a ruler of balance, now a tyrant of shadows, now a keeper who bears the weight of silence itself. Yet in all guises, he remains the eternal keeper of endings, his realm an inexhaustible well of meaning. This enduring legacy invites us to ask not only why the Underworld captivates us still, but also how these myths will shape the stories yet to come.

> *"There in the house of Hades, all must come,*
> *Shadows of what once was, bound by fate,*
> *And his rule shall endure for all eternity."*
> — Homer, *Odyssey*

Mystery of Death

Death has ever been humanity's most profound mystery, and the myths of the Underworld offered a sacred lens through which to glimpse what lies beyond. The Greeks imagined the afterlife not as heaven and hell, but as a layered cosmos—Elysium for the blessed, Tartarus for the damned, Asphodel for the countless dead who lingered in twilight—a reflection of moral complexity far subtler than the rigid heavens and hells that followed.

The Underworld also endures as a place of transformation. Again and again, mythic heroes descended into its depths and returned altered—Orpheus with grief, Heracles with triumph, Odysseus with wisdom, Aeneas with purpose. Their journeys through shadow revealed a truth as old as story itself that descent into darkness can yield new strength, and that confrontation with death, even in symbol, is a crucible of change. And still today, this theme echoes in modern tales, where passages through the Underworld serve as metaphors for struggle, growth, and self-discovery.

At the heart of this fascination stands Hades, the most enigmatic of Olympians. Unlike Zeus, who ruled the heavens, or Poseidon, who stirred the seas, Hades kept to a kingdom apart—his sovereignty absolute, his nature veiled. He was no oppressor, yet no savior, but a force of balance, ensuring the eternal rhythm of life and death. This ambiguity has allowed his figure to shift endlessly across ages. Sometimes villain, sometimes misunderstood warden, sometimes a solemn guardian of cosmic law. It is in this mystery, this refusal to be bound to a single role, that Hades remains inexhaustible—an eternal subject of awe, fear, and reverence in every age of storytelling. Yet even as myth gave voice to mystery, imagination gave it form—each age reshaping the realm of Hades in its own image.

Retold and Reborn

The myths of Hades kingdom have never fallen silent. They echo through the corridors of time, reshaped by each age of imagination. From Dante's infernal descent to the stories that flicker across page and screen today, the vision of a realm beyond life—where souls are judged, wandering, or reborn—remains one of humanity's most enduring symbols.

In literature, the Underworld serves as both mirror and crucible. Dante's *Inferno*, though framed in Christian theology, draws its order from Tartarus, where Sisyphus, Tantalus, and other transgressors endured endless trial. Modern voices—Rick Riordan, Neil Gaiman, Madeline Miller—continue that descent in new forms, reshaping Hades as weary sovereign, reluctant guardian, or god bound by love and solitude. Their retellings preserve the rivers, gates, and keepers of myth, yet render them intimate and human, alive to the questions of faith, justice, and mortality.

Cinema and television carry this fascination forward. From *Hercules* to *Blood of Zeus*, from *Supernatural* to *American Gods*, the Lord of the Dead endures as both shadow and mirror—sometimes villain, sometimes arbiter, sometimes the silence that waits beyond all things. Even in worlds of capes and gods, his dominion lingers. Wonder Woman's battles below, or Pluto beside Hel, remind us that every myth returns to death's threshold.

And still, the journey downward continues. The hero's passage through shadow—Orpheus, Aeneas, Heracles—finds reflection in modern figures who face loss, endure trial, and emerge transformed. In *Hades* and *God of War*, players descend as heroes themselves, crossing rivers once sung by poets. New frontiers—virtual, cinematic, and unseen—await their turn to reopen the gates.

Thus, the realm of Hades endures—its silence reborn in every age, its questions retold in every story. Myths of death and destiny do not fade. They transform, waiting always for the next soul brave enough to enter the dark and seek the light beyond.

CLOSING THE GATES OF THE DEAD

The myths of Hades and the Underworld have never remained bound to antiquity. They have changed their form yet kept their power—finding new voices in the verses of Dante, the frescoes of the Renaissance, the pages of modern fantasy, and the shimmering worlds of cinema and game. The god of the dead has worn many faces; villain and warden, judge and reluctant sovereign. His realm has become a stage for terror and transcendence alike, a mirror through which humanity contemplates its own end and its longing to remain relevant. From parchment to pixel, from temple song to digital screen, these tales prove inexhaustible—reflecting our eternal awe before death and the mystery beyond the veil.

As this descent draws to its end, it is fitting to pause and look upward—to consider what these myths have revealed of ourselves. The last chapter will gather what the journey has unearthed; the lessons of shadow, the weight of judgment, and the light that waits beyond the dark. As we depart the halls of Hades and ascend toward reflection, we carry with us what all ages have sought to know—that death is not silence, but story, for in every telling, Hades' shadow endures—and within that shadow, the light of myth still burns.

CHAPTER 13

END OF THE JOURNEY

Wandering in the Elysium Fields

Through ages uncounted, the myths of Hades and his Underworld have stirred the human imagination. They are not merely tales of gods and shades, but mirrors of the soul—speaking to our dread of death, our hunger for meaning, and our wonder before the unseen. In these stories, the realm below becomes both threshold and revelation. A place of judgment and renewal, where mortal life yields to mystery. To trace why these myths still command us is to glimpse their eternal power—the way they echo human hope and fear, transforming the end of life into the beginning of understanding.

> "No man may escape his fate,
> nor outrun the path set before him,
> For all must journey to the house of Hades,
> And there behold the mysteries beyond life."
> — Homer, *Iliad*

Where Gods and Mortals Meet

Greek mythology endures as one of humanity's most enduring storytelling legacies, shaping literature, art, and philosophy across the centuries. Unlike many faiths long fallen silent, these myths still breathe through us—reborn with every retelling, yet faithful to their ancient core. Their strength lies in the union of mortal and immortal.

The gods of Greece were not distant arbiters but reflections of the human heart—capable of jealousy, compassion, rage, and love. Hades, above all, stands apart; a sovereign bound by law rather than cruelty, guardian of balance rather than vengeance. He is stern but not merciless, embodying the certainty of death without the malice of destruction. In him, the divine and the human converge; his kingdom reveals both the finality and the fairness of existence.

The Greek vision of the afterlife was equally ordered and profound. It offered not chaos but structure—Tartarus for the condemned, Elysium for the blessed, and the Asphodel Meadows for the countless who linger between. This intricate design reflected the Greek devotion to balance and justice, ideals that still echo in modern storytelling. From novels to films to interactive worlds, the belief that deeds determine destiny continues to shape our imagination of what lies beyond.

Yet beyond philosophy and order, the myths endure because they are exquisite stories—tragic, radiant, and eternal. The Underworld sets the stage for love and loss, for valor and despair; Orpheus descending for Eurydice, Heracles wrestling Cerberus, Persephone drawn into shadow and spring. These tales remain luminous because they speak to the timeless pulse of longing and return. That we still see them reborn in film and literature proves their unbroken hold on the human spirit.

Hope at the Gates of Hades

Since the dawn of memory, humankind has turned to story to face the mystery of death. The Greek vision of Hades gave form to that fear—shaping it into images both terrible and tender. In this realm, mortality found meaning. Punishment for the cruel, reward for the just, and quiet shadow for those between.

The greatest terror was always finality—the thought that death ends all things. Yet Greek myth tempers this dread with the promise of renewal. Orphic hymns speak of rebirth; the descent and return of heroes suggest that death can be crossed; and Persephone's cycle between the worlds teaches that every winter yields to spring. These stories whisper that death is transformation, not annihilation.

Even within punishment there lies reflection. The agony of Sisyphus, the hunger of Tantalus, and the fall of Icarus are not cruelties but lessons—warnings against hubris, impatience, and excess. Achilles' brief glory asks a question that still lingers in every age. Is it nobler to burn bright and perish, or to endure and fade? In each, we find philosophy clothed in myth, and wisdom born of suffering.

Above all, these tales remind us that to live fully is to live with awareness of the end. The Underworld exists not to haunt us, but to make life sacred—to remind mortals that each act, each choice, echoes beyond the grave.

Eternal Descent and Return

The journey into Hades is among the oldest patterns in human storytelling. Descent, trial, and return. It is a metaphor for transformation, a mirror of life's own cycle of loss and renewal. Odysseus sought counsel, Orpheus love, Heracles redemption. Each returned changed, bearing insight forged in shadow.

In this descent we find the essence of human experience—the courage to face what must be faced. The rivers of the realm still flow through the modern soul; the Styx for oaths unbroken, Lethe for forgetting, Acheron for grief, Phlegethon for fury, Cocytus for lament. They are the inner currents of existence itself.

And at the center stands Hades—not villain nor savior, but inevitability given form. He reminds mortals that endings are not to be fled but understood. The Greeks did not cast him as evil, for they knew death as balance, not punishment. To accept his dominion is to embrace truth, that through every fall there is becoming, and through every ending, a return to order.

Enduring Reign of Myths

The myths of Hades endure because they illuminate what it means to live within the shadow of fate. They confront the oldest fear and transform it into understanding. The structured justice of the Greek afterlife still shapes the moral imagination of the West, while the compassion and restraint of Hades himself remind us that death is not chaos, but continuity.

So long as humankind wonders what lies beyond the veil, his kingdom will never fall silent. From the hymns of poets to the screens of our age, the Underworld persists as symbol and mirror—an eternal stage upon which the human spirit faces its destiny.

In that reflection lies the enduring truth. Death is not silence, but story. Every retelling rekindles the ancient flame, and in every age the shadow of Hades endures—proof that even in darkness, meaning survives.

RECKONING OF SOULS

The myths of Hades and the Underworld are not merely tales of gods, heroes, and the dead, but reflections of justice, destiny, and the eternal rhythm between life and death. Within their depths lie ancient truths about morality, the weight of choice, and the inevitability of fate. The judgment of souls, the renewal promised in Orphic tradition, and the unbending law of destiny reveal a cosmos ordered by consequence and bound by divine balance. These stories endure because they speak to what is timeless—the nature of existence, the measure of virtue, and the vast design in which every act resounds into eternity.

> "The deeds of men echo beyond the grave,
> For in the halls of Hades, justice waits,
> And none may flee the reckoning of fate."
> — Aeschylus, *Eumenides*

Scales of the Underworld

The Greek Underworld was never a void of chaos or despair, but a realm of divine order where every soul confronted the truth of its own life. Unlike the rigid heavens and hells of later faiths, it was a domain of balance, neither wholly cruel nor wholly merciful. Here, the dead were judged not by destiny alone but by the deeds that had defined them.

At its heart lay the Greek conviction that justice governs all things. Hades, though feared, was no tyrant but a keeper of equilibrium. His duty was solemn—to guard the threshold between worlds, to grant the dead their due, and to preserve the harmony that binds life and death. Where Zeus ruled the heavens and Poseidon commanded the sea, Hades held dominion over the inevitable. In him, mortality itself found its fairness.

The lesson remains enduring. Every deed bears consequence, and justice, however long delayed, cannot be escaped. The myths of the Underworld stand as both warning and mirror—reminding us that the choices made in life shape the shadows we leave behind.

Seasons of Shadow and Light

Though often imagined as final, the Greek Underworld was also a turning point in the eternal cycle—a passage of transformation rather than an end. Life and death were not adversaries but companions, two halves of a single rhythm that sustained the cosmos.

Foremost among these tales is that of Persephone—seized by Hades, yet destined to return. Her descent and ascent mark the world's breathing. The stillness of winter in her absence, the bloom of spring at her return. In her story, death becomes a season, a necessary silence before renewal.

The Orphic Mysteries deepened this truth, teaching that souls move through countless lifetimes, purified by death and reborn through knowledge until they ascend beyond the mortal cycle. Similar visions appear in distant lands—in Hindu and Buddhist thought—where the spirit journeys toward awakening through the wheel of existence.

Even the myth of Heracles and Alcestis speaks of death's impermanence. When Alcestis offered her life for her husband, Heracles, moved by her sacrifice, wrestled Thanatos himself and restored her to the living. In that defiance of fate lies a profound grace. Though all are bound by mortality, love and courage can momentarily unbind the thread.

These myths remind us that death is not a wall, but a doorway, and that every descent—whether of gods, heroes, or humankind—leads toward renewal.

Destiny Beyond Gods and Men

No idea in Greek thought stands higher than fate. The Moirai—the three ancient weavers of destiny—spun, measured, and cut the thread of every life, mortal or divine. Their decree was final; even the gods bowed before it. In Hades' realm, this truth reached completion, for there the threads were gathered, and destiny's design revealed its end.

To the Greeks, fate was not cruelty but order—the impartial law that binds existence. Even the mightiest could not outrun it. Achilles, nearly invincible, was fated to die young; his mother's desperate protection only sealed that truth. Oedipus, warned by prophecy, fled from doom only to meet it on the very road he took to escape. And in the *Iliad*, Zeus himself laments that he cannot save his beloved son Sarpedon from death, for not even the king of gods may unmake what the Fates have spun.

The message endures that destiny cannot be avoided, but it can be met with courage. The Greeks revered those who faced their appointed end with honor, and scorned those who defied it in arrogance. Sisyphus, who sought to cheat death, earned eternal futility. Yet those who accepted their fate—like Achilles, who chose brief glory over long obscurity—became immortal in story. In this, the Greeks found wisdom, that mortality is not a curse, but a canvas upon which greatness is painted.

Lessons from the Underworld

The myths of Hades endure because they illuminate life itself. In their shadows we see the order of justice, the promise of renewal, and the unyielding truth of fate. They teach that every act carries consequence, that death is but a passage, and that destiny—though immutable—can be met with grace.

Yet within that inevitability lies choice. Mortals cannot command their fates, but they can choose how to face them—with courage, humility, and reverence for the mystery that life itself represents. To walk through Hades' gate is not only to encounter death—it is to recognize the sacred pattern that unites beginning and end, shadow and light, mortal and divine.

So, the stories remain, not warnings alone, but wisdom preserved. In every age, they remind us that justice waits, that the soul endures, and that even in the darkness beneath the earth, meaning burns like an undying flame.

HADES IN OUR AGE

The myths of Hades and the Underworld have long outlived the mortals who first gave them voice. No longer confined to temple hymns or etched upon stone, they have endured through the ages, reshaped in books, on screens, and across every medium of art. Across centuries, Hades himself has shifted from distant sovereign to layered symbol—a god of order, introspection, and the mysteries that bind life to death. Today, the Underworld is not merely the resting place of souls, but a vast stage where stories of trial, transformation, and redemption unfold. Greek mythology has not fallen silent; it lives anew, its shadows still guiding the imagination of our age.

> *"The Underworld is not a place of mere darkness,*
> *But a realm where truth is revealed,*
> *And the souls of the dead find their destined place."*
> — Virgil, *Aeneid*

Stories Woven Anew

Greek mythology continues to cast its spell across modern storytelling. The Underworld, once a land of myth and mystery, now reappears as a realm of challenge, reflection, and transcendence. Writers, filmmakers, and game creators draw deeply from these ancient wells, translating their truths for new generations while preserving their eternal resonance.

Among the most celebrated reimaginings is Rick Riordan's *Percy Jackson & The Olympians*, where the Underworld rises again as a vast subterranean dominion ruled by a complex, weary god. Charon ferries the dead across the Styx, the Asphodel Meadows drift in eternal twilight, and Hades himself emerges neither as villain nor savior, but as a dignified, misunderstood ruler. This portrayal signals a broader shift in modern mythmaking—away from rigid morality toward humanized divinity.

Video games, too, have given myth a new heartbeat. *Supergiant Games' Hades* (2020) reimagines the legend through Zagreus, the rebellious son of the god of the dead, seeking escape from his father's realm. Here, Hades stands as stern yet paternal—a figure of structure, not cruelty—while his kingdom unfolds in immersive splendor; Tartarus of trial, Asphodel of fire, Elysium of grace. Through play, mortals now walk paths once sung by poets, turning ancient legend into living experience.

Cinema likewise returns again and again to Hades' dominion. Disney's *Hercules* (1997) recast him as a sharp-tongued schemer, imprinting a mischievous image on popular culture. *Clash of the Titans* (2010) and its sequel painted him darker still—a rival to Zeus, forged from wrath and exile. Yet whether rendered with humor or dread, each portrayal affirms the same truth. The god of the dead still commands the screen, his myths forever reborn in light and shadow.

Hidden Heart of Hades

Among the most striking transformations in modern retellings is the emergence of Hades not as a specter of fear, but as a figure of empathy and depth. In antiquity, he was a distant arbiter, cold but impartial—a force of necessity. In modern hands, he becomes something more. A god of burden and restraint, torn between duty and desire, his solitude touched by humanity.

This shift reflects our age's fascination with flawed divinity. Works such as Madeline Miller's *Circe* portray gods not as archetypes, but as beings capable of tenderness and doubt. Rachel Smythe's acclaimed webcomic *Lore Olympus* transforms the abduction of Persephone into a nuanced romance, where Hades stands as a reserved yet compassionate ruler, concealing gentleness behind solemn order. Through such portrayals, he becomes a mirror for the modern spirit—powerful yet uncertain, just yet longing to be understood.

This evolution speaks to a larger cultural awakening. Once, death was depicted as terror; now it is viewed as balance. The Underworld becomes not damnation, but reflection—a realm where endings are recognized as beginnings in disguise. In this new vision, Hades embodies not horror, but harmony. A sovereign who reminds the living that mortality gives life its shape and meaning.

Even beyond the written word, this reinterpretation continues to spread. In television and animation—such as Netflix's *Blood of Zeus* (2020)—Hades appears not as pure villain, but as a being of restraint and conviction, his ambitions tempered by duty. This trend reveals the pulse of modern mythmaking. Audiences seek gods who bear the weight of conscience, who rule not by fear but by purpose. Through this lens, Hades endures not as shadow, but as reflection—a presence to be contemplated rather than feared.

Myth in Literature and Art

The Underworld has always been a theater of revelation—a place where the unseen becomes known, where souls and stories alike pass through transformation. In modern art and literature, that ancient descent continues, reshaped for the age of reason and imagination.

In literature, the passage through darkness remains an enduring motif. Neil Gaiman's *The Sandman* and Stephen King's *The Dark Tower* echo the structure of the ancient katabasis—the descent into shadow to retrieve truth or redemption. Even in works beyond mythology, the journey into darkness endures as metaphor for grief, self-discovery, and transcendence, proving that the pathways to Hades are still walked in the human imagination.

Cinema, too, continues this dialogue with death and rebirth. Films such as *Coco* (2017) and *Soul* (2020) explore the afterlife through cultural lenses far from Greece, yet their emotional core remains the same; memory endures, choices matter, and the spirit moves onward. These stories reaffirm that though beliefs may differ, humanity's longing to understand what lies beyond the veil unites all peoples.

In art, the Underworld has never ceased to inspire. Where ancient potters painted Charon's ferry and Cerberus' gate, modern creators—painters, sculptors, and digital artists—reinterpret the abyss as both beauty and meditation. Some envision vast shadowed kingdoms; others depict Hades and Persephone in quiet grace. Each brushstroke, each rendered form, continues the dialogue begun millennia ago, proving that the myths of the dead remain among the most vital expressions of life.

FROM MYTH TO MODERNITY

The myths of Hades and the Underworld have shown rare endurance, reshaping themselves to meet the imagination of every new age. From books and films to games and webcomics, these ancient tales continue to inspire, evolving into new forms while preserving their eternal core. Hades himself has transformed across centuries—from distant and feared sovereign to complex, burdened figure, an antihero whose gravity commands both respect and empathy. Meanwhile, the Underworld remains an endless stage upon which humanity wrestles with its oldest questions; fate, justice, and the unseen mysteries beyond mortal life.

As long as mortals ponder the meaning of existence and the shadow that follows, the myths of Hades will not perish. Whether carved in stone, written in verse, or rendered in pixels of light, the ruler of the dead endures as guardian of story and symbol. Standing at the threshold of myth and modernity, Hades remains eternal—a reminder that even in darkness, purpose abides, and from the depths of shadow, the light of meaning forever rises.

EPILOGUE

LEGACY OF THE
UNSEEN KING

Sovereign of the Silent Realm

Among the most ancient and enduring figures of Greek myth, Hades remains both feared and revered—a god whose presence has not faded with the centuries, but deepened in meaning. Unlike his brothers who ruled sky and sea, Hades reigned in silence, unseen by mortal eyes. His dominion was the one realm no soul could enter and return unchanged, and for that reason his power carried a permanence beyond conquest or ceremony. He was not merely lord of the dead, but guardian of fate, keeper of mysteries, and sentinel of the truth that all mortals must one day face.

Hades' strength endures in his balance. He waged no wars, sought no temples, and demanded no songs. His sovereignty was marked not by ambition but by inevitability—a reign of restraint, not conquest. With quiet finality, he upheld the boundary between life and death, ensuring order where chaos might have reigned. Mortals trembled at his name, yet they respected the justice he preserved, for his kingdom was ruled not by cruelty, but by necessity.

The Underworld itself reflected that same equilibrium. Unlike the rigid dualities of later heavens and hells, Hades' kingdom formed a vast tapestry of realms, the drifting meadows of Asphodel, the radiant fields of Elysium, and the abyssal depths of Tartarus. These places did not divide souls by absolutes of good or evil, but weighed them by the measure of their lives. Within that vision lay an ancient wisdom—that humankind is neither wholly pure nor wholly corrupt, and that true justice must mirror the complexity of the mortal heart.

Through the myths of Orpheus and Eurydice, and through Persephone's descent and return, the Underworld became more than a destination. It became a metaphor for all cycles of love, loss, consequence, and renewal. Mortality found its meaning there, and death its voice. In these stories, silence itself speaks—of transformation, of balance, of truths that lie beyond fear.

Even now, Hades endures in art, literature, and imagination—not as tyrant or demon, but as a symbol of order, purpose, and the eternal rhythm of existence. In him, the ancient Greeks placed their dread, and through him they discovered wisdom. His tale is not of darkness, but of understanding—the last sentinel who does not end the story, but completes it.

This is the legacy of the unseen king.

> *"May those who walk the path of shadows*
> *Find the light that guides beyond the veil,*
> *For the soul is never lost, only transformed."*
> — *Orphic Hymn to Hades*

ABOUT THE AUTHOR

Seeker of Stories, Weaver of Myth

Michael J. Defosse is a published author with a background in the business world and a passion for storytelling. He holds an undergraduate degree in Economics and two graduate degrees from Syracuse University, bringing a unique blend of analytical thinking and creative inspiration to his work. His previous books, primarily focused on finance and risk management, showcased his expertise in his professional field. However, his love for mythology, folklore, and fantasy has guided him toward a new literary adventure.

Growing up in a small town surrounded by nature, Michael spent his childhood exploring the forest behind his home and fishing in the nearby lake. These early experiences fostered a deep connection with the natural world, allowing his imagination to wander through the myths and legends of ancient cultures. The quiet of the woods and the mysteries of the lake often brought to mind the stories of gods, heroes, and mythical creatures that would later inspire his writing.

With his new five-book series on Greek mythology, Michael combines his lifelong love of mythology with his talent for storytelling. Each book in the series invites readers to explore the ancient world, bringing the timeless tales of the Greek gods and their adventures to life. Michael hopes his stories will ignite the imaginations of readers of all ages, much as his own imagination was sparked by his childhood walks in the forest.

Greek Mythology: Dominion of Poseidon

Myths of Sea Gods, Ocean Monsters, and Ancient Legends of the Deep

Venture beyond the shadowed gates of the Underworld and rise to the restless seas—where power, creation, and chaos move as one.

In this sweeping third volume of the *Greek Mythology* series by Michael J Defosse, the dominion of Poseidon unfolds in all its might. Journey through coral palaces and tempest-ridden waters to meet the god who rules both calm and storm—the Earthshaker, the Builder of Atlantis, and the eternal master of the deep.

Discover how Poseidon's trident shaped lands, birthed horses, and split the world itself. Encounter nymphs and monsters born of the abyss, from the prophetic Proteus to the fearsome Scylla. Walk among lost civilizations claimed by the sea—Helike, Atlantis, and other sunken realms where divine wrath met mortal pride.

Through mythic prose and vivid illustration, *Dominion of Poseidon* explores the eternal duality of the sea. Its beauty, its terror, and its power to both cradle and destroy civilizations. This is the story of a god whose mood could shake the earth—and whose name still echoes in every crashing wave.

Where the deep is not silence—but the voice of the divine.

Available soon on Amazon and wherever books from Mythology Publishing are sold.

Continue the Journey
www.MythologyPublishing.com

Thank You for Joining Me on This Journey!

We hope you enjoyed *Greek Mythology: Kingdom of Hades* and found it both interesting and insightful. Your thoughts matter to us, and your book review can make a significant difference by helping other readers discover this book.

Share Your Thoughts!

If you enjoyed this book, please consider leaving a review on Amazon or your favorite book review site. Your feedback will not only guide future readers but also support me in creating even better content for upcoming publications.

How to Leave a Review on Amazon:

1. **Visit the Book Page:**

Go to the *Greek Mythology: Kingdom of Hades* product page on Amazon.

2. **Sign In:**

Make sure you're logged into your Amazon account.

3. **Share Your Thoughts:**

- Scroll down to the **Customer Reviews** section.
- Click the **Write a Customer Review** button.
- Share what you loved about the book—whether it was the stories, the mythology, or the characters.

Your Opinion Matters!

Your honest review not only helps other readers but also enables me to continue bringing the fascinating world of mythology to life.

Stay in Touch!

I'd love to hear more from you. If you have additional comments or thoughts, feel free to reach out directly at **info@mythologypublishing.com**.

Thank you for being part of this mythological journey!

Sincerely,

Michael J. Defosse